Funny About Love

A comedy

Terence Frisby

Samuel French — London
New York - Toronto - Hollywood

FUNNY ABOUT LOVE

First presented at Yvonne Arnaud Theatre, Guildford, by
Paul Farrah Productions in association with the Yvonne
Arnaud Theatre, Guildford, and the Theatre Royal,
Windsor, on 18th May 1999 with the following cast of
characters:

Rosie Boston	Stephanie Beacham
Darren Tucker	Sean Maguire
Piers Boston	Robert East
Larissa Tucker	Sarah Wittuck

Designed by Julie Godfrey
Lighting by Douglas Kuhrt

CHARACTERS

Rosie Boston
Darren Tucker
Piers Boston
Larissa Tucker

The action takes place in the Bostons' London flat

Time—the present

SYNOPSIS OF SCENES

ACT I
  SCENE 1 An early evening in October, just before sunset
  SCENE 2 The following evening

ACT II
  SCENE 1 An early evening the following May
  SCENE 2 Later the same evening
  SCENE 3 Dawn the following morning

AUTHOR'S NOTE

I have given an alternative ending on page 67 and a few alternative lines (in square brackets) in this published version of the play.

The alternative ending was not tried in the original production, but it has the merit that it ties up the final thread of the story, which is otherwise left floating, so could well be the more satisfying. I look forward to seeing it performed one day.

Nicky Henson, who directed the play at the Chichester Festival Theatre for the second tour, and all the original cast made valuable contributions to the final text and I thank them, particularly Robert East, an author himself, who was most inventive.

Terence Frisby

Other plays by Terence Frisby published by Samuel French Ltd

Rough Justice
There's a Girl in my Soup

ACT I
SCENE 1

The Bostons' London flat. October, early evening

It is a spacious, stylish flat on the river, either in Docklands, Chelsea or Fulham. In addition to the front door, there are doors to the kitchen and two bedrooms. There is a four-legged dining-table reasonably prominent on the set and two framed paintings by Turner, his late period, very impressionistic. Other furniture includes a sofa and coffee table. N.B. it is suggested that, for lighting and dramatic reasons, the main window of the room (through which the sunrise shines in Act II, SCENE 3) is set in a side wall of the set rather than upstage. It is daylight outside, fading to evening later in the scene

Rosie is sitting, shoes off, C with a half-finished TV dinner at her feet. She is listening to classical music on her CD player

The door entryphone rings. Rosie gets up and puts her shoes on as the entryphone rings again. She picks up her TV dinner, switches off the CD, crosses to the entryphone and answers it

Rosie Hallo? … Speaking. … Delivery? A bit late, isn't it? … Oh, all right. First floor.

She presses the door-release button and hangs up. She goes and unbolts the top and bottom bolts on her front door and opens the door, which is still on the security chain

   She takes her TV dinner off to the kitchen

   Darren's face appears in the gap of the front door

Darren (*calling through the gap*) Hallo? Mrs Boston?
Rosie (*off*) Yes, here. Can you put it through?
Darren Er — no, it's too big.

   Rosie enters

Rosie What is it?

Darren A package.
Rosie Well, do I have to sign for it or something?
Darren Yes.
Rosie Can't you shove that through?
Darren Oh. Yeah. Here. (*His hand pushes through a clipboard with pen attached. His second hand comes through and points at it*) Just there, please.
Rosie (*curious*) Photographic and reproduction studios? (*The official look of the board reassures her as she signs it, then, releases the chain and opens the front door. Relaxed*) What's all this? I haven't ordered anything photographic?

She hands Darren the clipboard and receives from him a nice, plastic, one-bottle carrier bag with a ribbon on top and a card attached

Darren There you are, Mrs Boston. It says it all on the card.

She turns away from the door to switch on the lights to read it. As she does so, Darren slips into the room. Darren Tucker is young and downmarket; normally cocky he is now unsure of himself, quite nervous in fact. He is dressed in cheap, well-worn probably grubby cycling gear, with helmet, mask or handkerchief to breathe through and rucksack; perhaps old or torn jeans

Rosie "For us to drink together." Who's us?
Darren (*closing the door*) You and me.
Rosie (*startled*) What? I didn't say you could come in.
Darren It's all right. Don't worry. I'm quite safe. No bother. I just want to have a talk.
Rosie What about?
Darren I'm your husband's secretary's husband.
Rosie What?
Darren (*slower*) Your husband's secretary's husband.
Rosie My husband's secretary's ...? Ooh.
Darren That's right.
Rosie Good heavens. (*Pause*) Well, what do you want?
Darren Just to meet you.
Rosie Whatever for?
Darren Dunno, really ... Well ... I suppose I wanted to know ... (*He is struggling with his feelings*) How do *you* feel about your old man buggering off with my missus.

And having got that out he relaxes a little and feels a little more in charge. Pause. Rosie looks at him, still unsure

Rosie (*cautiously*) Whose missus she is doesn't affect how I feel about it.

Darren is disappointed that his firework is merely a damp squib

Darren Oh. No. S'pose not really.
Rosie Actually, it never occurred to me that she was *anyone's* missus.
    I just thought of her as some little bit of ... I don't see why marriage
    should raise her status in my mind but ... What prejudices one has. So.
    Here you are, the other part of the equation, the other dumpee.
Darren Come again?
Rosie Dumpee. Haven't you been discarded as well?
Darren Oh. Yeah. Funny, innit?
Rosie Funny?
Darren I meant this — us. Standing here.
Rosie Rollicking. Perhaps you'd better sit down.
Darren Cheers. (*He doesn't move*)
Rosie As you wish. (*Pause*) I always think that's a ghastly expression,
    don't you?
Darren What?
Rosie Cheers.
Darren What?
Rosie Cheers is such a frightful expression, unless you're drinking, of
    course. But as a substitute for thank you ...

She sees that this is all beyond Darren

    Oh, well, it seems it's here to stay.

Darren takes the bottle of champagne from the bag and holds it out

Darren 'S cold. 'S all ready to drink. I got it from the cold cabinet in the
    supermarket. (*He holds out the bottle*)
Rosie (*with eyebrows raised*) Cremant de Bourgogne?
Darren 'S like champagne, only cheaper.
Rosie Trying to impress me, were you?
Darren (*concerned*) No, no. 'S only cheaper in price, not in quality.
    Rissa always gets it.
Rosie Rissa?
Darren Yeah. My — my ... *her.*
Rosie Is that her name? Rissa?
Darren Short for Larissa.
Rosie Ah. Well, well. I named her Open-Legs-Annie. I suppose you'd
    better uncork that, I'll get some glasses.

During the following he removes the foil and half undoes the wire and takes a paper napkin from his rucksack which he lays over his forearm so that he ends up waiting for her, looking like a waiter

Darren You know what I call *him*? Ferret Face.
Rosie Yes, very good.

She holds the glasses before him but he motions her to set them down. He removes the wire, holds the cork and twists the bottle, precisely according to the book. As the cork comes out he quickly pours, holding each glass tilted so that it will not foam over. All is deftly done, a little ceremony. He offers her a glass and keeps one

I see you've been trained to do all that very neatly.
Darren Yeah.
Rosie } *(together)* { Rissa? Yes.
Darren }   { Rissa. Yeah.
Rosie *(raising her glass)* Well. To ...
Darren What, then?
Rosie Rissa and Piers.
Darren Eh?
Rosie Ferret Face and Open-Legs-Annie. Sod 'em both.
Darren *(overlapping)* Up theirs.

They drink

What d'you think of it?
Rosie Very nice. Thank you. But I have had it before. Your dear, evangelical Rissa obviously converted Piers to it.

Darren doesn't understand evangelical nor punctilious

Darren Yeah. Well.
Rosie And Piers, punctilious as always that I should miss none of the new-found pleasures of life that he was experiencing, brought home a *crate* of it.
Darren She said he always bought them champagne. She'd kissed the old Cremant goodbye.
Rosie How one warms to her. The girl friend gets the champagne, the wife gets the Cremant. God, he's antediluvian, isn't he?
Darren Anti what?
Rosie Sorry. It's from the Latin: ante, before; diluvian, the flood.
Darren What flood's that?
Rosie The biggie. Noah's Ark and all that.

Darren Nohzark?
Rosie Not nohzark. Noah's Ark.
Darren (*blankly*) Oh, yeah, yeah. Course. Cheers.

Rosie winces

Rosie Didn't you do all that at school, in religious instruction?
Darren Religious instruction? At my school? Listen, the Muslims wouldn't come to our religious classes, we wouldn't go the Muslims, the Jews held their own and the Catholics brought notes from their mum.

Rosie stares at him for a while

Rosie What gulfs there are between us.
Darren You don't have to take the piss.
Rosie I was thinking of Rissa and ... (*She smiles*) Poor Piers. What has he done this time?
Darren (*suddenly singing*) "The animals went in two by two, parlez-vous." Is that it?
Rosie (*laughing*) Thank God we've found a cultural point of reference.
Darren I never learned no Latin.
Rosie Or English, it seems.
Darren Or religion, or history, or any of that old stuff and you just go on taking the piss. But I'm learning now.
Rosie Splendid. So the area of your ignorance will shrink and fewer people will be able to take the piss from you in future.

There is a simmering, resentful pause

Darren Anyway, why is Ferret Face anti — whatever-it-was?
Rosie Er, excuse me, but let's get this completely straight — for the sake of clarity, not to take the ... I didn't say anti, I said ante. Anti with an i means against — that's Latin, too, by the way; ante, with an e means before. They are easily confused. There. A further shrinkage — not a major one, but nevertheless.

Darren manages to accept this

Darren Right. Cheers.
Rosie Let's have another drink.
Darren Right. My name's Darren, by the way. Everyone calls me Daz... some call me Dazza.

Rosie Darren will do fine.

Darren Darren Tucker.

Rosie Ah, that's her surname, is it? Rissa Tucker. I'm Rosie.

Darren Rosie Boston.

Rosie Precisely.

Darren You're not what I expected.

Rosie Ah, well, that's life.

Darren I mean, well, your old man, he's such a boring-looking, old fart — if you don't mind me saying.

Rosie No.

Darren And you, well, you're — quite — nice.

Rosie Easy on.

Darren's resentment pours out

Darren You know when you get married — I mean — you know it might not all go smoothly, you can expect *anything*. But *him. That. Ferret Face.* I mean — the humiliation, I come home from work dead tired, and he's in there with her. No supper, Ferret Face's eating it. I wasn't even allowed through the front door. He's in, you're out. I've packed your stuff. Here it is. Goodbye.

Rosie Didn't you put up a fight?

Darren She kept him out the way. I didn't even see him.

Rosie No, I didn't mean punch him — though you're welcome — I meant why didn't you fight for your wife, your marriage?

Darren Oh. She'd made up her mind. I know her.

Rosie Such determination. You know, that shit of a husband of mine phoned me after I — after I found out about them. He asked me to move out of here so that they could move in. I told him where to go.

Darren (*resentfully*) Yeah. My place.

Rosie But you didn't even try to save your place.

Darren Anyway, it was her place, not mine. She owned it.

Rosie Ah. Where?

Darren Maisonette in Potters Bar. I mean, what's your old man got that I haven't?

Rosie Yes, from your point of view he's not exactly — but women have always liked him.

Darren I made a bad mistake, you know. I told me mates. One of 'em said he'd have helped me out with Rissa if I couldn't, you know. So I hit him. Whack. Right in the eye.

Rosie You hit the wrong person.

Darren I'll say. He laid me out.

Rosie (*laughing*) I caught them at it, you know.

Darren What?

Rosie Yes.

Darren (*shocked*) At it?

Rosie In his office. I walked in, unannounced, one lunchtime and there they were. Across his desk.

Rosie You mean actually shagging?

Rosie It's wonderful how these words go full circle, isn't it? I remember saying "shagging" to my mother when I was about fourteen. She had fifty fits. Then shagging disappeared for a whole generation. We always screwed. Then bonking came in. Horrid. Now shagging is everywhere again, etymologically speaking.

Darren (*can't handle it*) They were shagging? On his desk?

Rosie That's why I called her Open-Legs-Annie.

Darren And you walked in just expecting to have lunch with your old man?

Rosie (*laughing involuntarily*) An open sandwich, actually.

Darren Coh, you must have been surprised.

Rosie No. They were surprised; I was astonished.

Darren What?

Rosie Sorry, sorry. An old joke, very old indeed.

Darren (*outraged*) How can you joke about your husband shagging someone else? Don't you care?

Rosie I'm not sure. (*And she really isn't*) The sight of those two little faces, one upside down, gawping at me across the office, made me — well — perhaps the laugh was only nervousness. He said — (*she laughs again*) see? I'm still at it — he said, "I wasn't expecting you". (*She shrugs*) Well. I said, "Your last words will be, I'm dying." He said, "Caustic as ever." I left. I mean, trust Piers ... *his secretary.*

Darren (*a cry of pain*) She's *my wife.*

Rosie Yes, sorry.

Darren It's like me doing it with — with my mother or someone.

Rosie You bring unexpected perspectives, don't you?

Darren Are you taking the piss again?

Rosie (*sharply*) Out of *myself*, you egocentric — (*she pulls herself together but her anger bubbles on*) out of *me.* I'm trying to absorb the cliché that my cultured, erudite, loving husband of twenty-two years has dumped me for a semi-savage, ignorant, allegedly attractive — but especially young — bit of arse. Then you come in here and tell me in your fluent little way that the reverse procedure would be unthinkable, almost incestuous.

Darren I think what *they've* done is disgusting, too.

Rosie Ah, well, that makes everything all right, of course. No double standards for Daz-The-New-Man.

Pause

Darren I think you've got a bit of a problem, you know.

Rosie I beg your pardon?

Darren An attitude problem. I don't just mean about Rissa 'n' your old man. I'm having trouble coming to terms with that myself, so I understand. No, I mean you seem to have a problem about everybody. Even me. I think you should have a bit of self-assessment, a bit of a re-think. It might help.

Rosie is surprised at this

You think everyone's thicker than you, including your old man. You think I am, Rissa is.

Rosie I've never met Rissa.

Darren See?

Rosie (*laughing, caught*) So, is delivering packages really what you do for a living?

Darren It's only temporary. I'm a student really.

Rosie Ah.

Darren I bike stuff for a photographic and reproduction studio to pay for my classes: Business Management and Law. I'm going to get a management and law diploma. Evening school and Open University. I'm trying to improve myself. (*He stares, perhaps even glares, at her for a moment*) Aren't you gonna say "there's room for it".

Rosie (*smiling*) No. I think that's admirable. Good luck to you.

Darren At least I'm making the journey.

Rosie Ah, yes, that journey that everyone's making.

Darren See? Pisstaking again.

Rosie Look, Darren, I don't really see any point in our swapping insults ten minutes after we've met just because your Rissa has bedazzled my Piers. So why don't you get on your bike and deliver some stuff?

Darren (*sitting back into his seat; he has no intention of going*) I'm done for the day.

Rosie And you've pedalled all the way from Potters Bar just to say hallo to me?

Darren No, no, I been dossing on a mate's floor in Muswell Hill.

Rosie Why have you come here?

Darren I just wanted to … Anyway, *you're* all right, aren't you. (*He looks round*) You got this place.

Rose picks up and waves a letter

Rosie I've just received this from his solicitor. Today. Piers wants this place back. He's drawn the balance from our joint bank account and refused responsibility for any future overdraft. If I write out a cheque now it'll bounce and he's cancelled all the joint credit cards.

Darren Use cash.

Rosie I've got seventeen pounds fifty in my bag. How do I eat?

Darren What? Seventeen quid'll feed you for days.

Rosie Such foresight.

Darren Where are your kids?

Rosie We don't have any.

Darren Why's that, then?

Rosie We couldn't, if you must know.

Darren Who was that, then? Him or you?

Rosie Mind your own bloody business.

Darren Sorry, sorry. I didn't mean … sorry, really.

Rosie Never mind. Just go.

Darren Well, ain't you got a job? Oh, no, I suppose …

Rosie (*offended*) What?

Darren We-ell, you wouldn't ever've needed one, would you?

Rosie Soft, little, pampered cow that I am.

Darren No, I didn't — sorry.

Rosie My rage at all this is *because* of my jobs. I don't want to lose them.

Darren Then you've got some money.

Rosie No, I haven't.

Darren What do you mean?

Rosie They're not the sort of jobs you get paid for.

Darren What d'you do 'em for, then?

Rosie They're not just jobs, they're my life. I work two days a week on environmental research — in other words I try to slow down the rate at which we're screwing up the world.

Darren (*not impressed*) For nothing.

Rosie (*fiercely*) It's wonderful. And I work two days a week for Amnesty International.

Darren (*uncertain*) Oh, yeah, yeah.

Rosie You don't know who they are, do you?

Darren (*assertively*) Yeah, course I do. (*Losing confidence*) They're them travel agents, ain't they?

Rosie I help get people out of prison.

Darren (*surprised*) Oh.

Rosie Innocent people.

Darren (*with a little laugh*) Well, they're all that in there, ain't they?

Rosie People with principles, in hell-holes all over the world.

Darren You like suffering, doncha?

Rosie (*giving up*) I'll give you some of our literature.

Darren And you *love* fighting. That's 'cos you've never had to do neither.

Rosie If I get wiped off the world this minute at least I will have done something worthwhile. I used to get paid. Quite well, actually.

Darren Doing what?

Rosie I was an investment adviser. Huh. Earning money for people who already had plenty. Now I have found two jobs that consume me I'm not losing them just because he wants to shag Open-Legs-Ann——oh, sorry.

Darren No, no. 'S all right. Go on. 'S interesting.

Rosie And I'm not losing my home either.

Darren Then sell something.

Rosie I've got nothing to sell.

Darren gestures and looks round him expressively

Darren Look at this stuff. One bit of furniture'll feed you for months. (*He indicates the Turners*) Even these old things must be worth something.

Rosie My God, the Turners. They're worth a fortune.

Darren What, them?

Rosie They've been in Piers' family for generations.

Darren Keep 'em.

Rosie But they're his.

Darren They're yours as well. You're his wife.

Rosie He'll be back for them.

Darren Don't let him in.

Rosie What?

Darren You heard.

Rosie But he — it's his flat too.

Darren They slung *me* out. They want to chuck you out. Change the locks.

Rosie I can't do that.

Darren I bloody would.

Rosie I don't know a locksmith.

Darren Yellow Pages. Now.

Rosie Of course. How stupid of me. (*She looks for the Yellow Pages, finds them, then searches in them*)

Darren (*indicating a painting*) Can I take this down? (*He does so*)

Rosie Be careful. Piers'll have a fit.

Darren Bit wishy-washy, aren't they? (*He examines the front and back of the painting*)

Rosie Wishy-washy? Turner? He was wonderful, unearthly. He beat the Impressionists to it by years. He loved the Thames. Just look at the light out of the window. There he is. (*Referring to the locksmiths section of* Yellow Pages) There are hundreds of them.

Darren peers out but is lost

Darren (*looking at the second painting*) So what are these worth?

Rosie God knows.

Darren Roughly, then.

Rosie They're insured for one-point-three each. Here we are, locksmith. Just round the corner.

Darren One-point-three? What's that mean?

Rosie Million. But that may be above their real value at auction; say one each to be sure.

Darren (*awestruck*) One-point-three million pounds?

Rosie Yes.

He lets out an involuntary exclamation

(*Irritated*) Don't do that. I'll lose the number.

The door entryphone rings, an idiosyncratic ring which Rosie recognizes

Darren Each? Bloody hell ... I'll drop it ... I'll put it back.

Darren re-hangs the painting as Rosie looks out of the window

Bloody hell.

Rosie (*to Darren*) It's Piers.

Darren Who?

Rosie Piers.

Darren Ferret Face?

Rosie He's coming up. (*She puts the chain on the door*) Quick. Hide.

Darren What for?

Rosie I don't know. Instinct.

Darren OK.

Rosie (*pushing him off*) Go on. In there.

Rosie ushers Darren into the bedroom, with his rucksack and helmet, as Piers opens the door with a key

Piers (*through the door gap*) Rosie?

Rosie (*off*) Yes. Just coming.
Piers You all right?
Rosie (*off*) Yes, yes. Hang on.

She enters and releases the chain and opens the door

Piers comes into the room

Piers Putting the chain on now, are we?
Rosie You notice everything, as always.
Piers You had a break-in or something?
Rosie That's what living on your own does for you.
Piers (*determined not to rise; agreeably*) Ah. That'll teach me.
Rosie To what do I owe the pleasure? Got an eviction order in your back pocket, have you?
Piers (*ploughing pleasantly on*) No, no, no, Rosie. Really. I just wanted to ——
Rosie You've never "just wanted to" anything in your whole life.

Piers laughs gently, buying the rebuke. He doesn't rise to Rosie at all

Piers You don't realize how much you miss someone until you hear them in action again.
Rosie Oh, dear. Compliments. Watch out.
Piers That's what I mean.
Rosie That's a really shitty letter from Shyster 'n' Screwyou or whoever they are.
Piers No, it's not, Rosie, and you know it. It's perfectly reasonable and it's why I'm here.
Rosie Unannounced.
Piers Do I have to announce myself to come home?
Rosie Home? Ha. It's *home* again, is it?
Piers I knew you'd be all up, in this mood. That's why I came. So come down, we have to talk; we can't go on pussyfooting about like we have been.
Rosie I need some money. Cash. Now.
Piers How much?
Rosie What?
Piers Will two hundred tide you over?
Rosie Well ...
Piers Here's three. There.
Rosie Oh.

Piers has noticed the bottle and glasses as he puts £300 down

Piers Is somebody here?
Rosie (*jumping*) What?

Piers points at the glasses

Rosie Oh. Oh, Jane was. Jane Crabtree.
Piers Oh.
Rosie Jane's alone, too. Ivor's left her. Not for his secretary. For God.
Piers (*half-laughing*) Jesus.
Rosie No, a more oriental version, I think. Gongs and robes and things.
Piers Do I get a glass?
Rosie You know where they are. This is your Home.

He gets himself a glass

Piers I thought you said Cremant was slop.
Rosie Of course, you love it, don't you? The discerning Rissa has led
   you to it, like a horse to water. Or was it a lamb to the slaughter?
Piers Where did you get Rissa from?
Rosie What?
Piers Rissa! Where d'you get that from?
Rosie I thought you said Larissa was her name.
Piers But you said Rissa.
Rosie La-rissa. The hearing going too, is it? I hope everything else is
   standing the strain.
Piers Look, Rosie, I just want to get things settled.
Rosie Pressing you a bit, is she, your tungsten-tipped fluffy bunny?
Piers The thing is, I'm not really making any money; the company is not
   declaring a dividend this year; and you've only got those tinpot jobs
   with Amnesty and Greenpeace.
Rosie (*dangerously*) Leave my jobs out of this.
Piers Yes, yes, I know, I'm privileged to subsidize such exemplary
   causes, but at the moment there are two homes, two lots of bills, and
   I've no real income. I'm living in a — a — well, a modest place — it's
   fine but it won't do for ——
Rosie And where is this modest place of yours?
Piers (*an embarrassed smile*) Potters Bar.
Rosie (*smiling*) Not quite your stamping ground.
Piers A tiny maisonette. Sweet. It's quite handy in some ways, just off
   the M25; exit 24.
Rosie So, what do we call you now? The Potters Bar Turn-Off?
Piers (*laughing emptily*) Oh, Rosie. You're taking all this very well. But
   I'm afraid that you might be thinking, if you just let all this drag on, I'll
   get tired of her and come home, don't you? That's the short of it.

Rosie lets out an involuntary gasp of indignation

No, no, I don't go as far as to say you *hope* I will. Perhaps you don't even care much by now, and I wouldn't blame you but, well, let's face it, it would suit you, wouldn't it? Well, look at the facts: we've got along fine for years but it's been sort of — well moribund, really, hasn't it? Oh, friendly, even affectionate, but not exactly vibrant since we gave up trying to have children. And it's always been me who's been the restless one, who's sought something — well, I mean, I know I've gone out and had the odd — well, affair and so on along the ... and it's you that's been contented to just let things ... and I don't blame you, very cosy. So naturally you'd prefer the status ... and I respect that, but this time it's different, I'm afraid. Sorry darling, but we have to ... and that's about it.

Pause

Rosie That is the most moving and original account of the break-up of a marriage that it has ever been my privilege to listen to.
Piers Rosie.
Rosie I just wish I'd taped it to fire into space for alien species to marvel at the beauty and profundity of the human spirit.
Piers Oh, Rosie, I wish you could feel as fulfilled as I do. Let's face it, Rosie, we've been dead for years, you and me. Now I've found — well — joy; true, full, rounded happiness. It's worth the upset. It is, really, I assure you.
Rosie (*nodding sympathetically*) Bit of a goer, is she?
Piers That side of life is ... well, wonderful.
Rosie That side of life. What a poet you are, Piers. Still at it across the office desk, are you?
Piers God, that was embarrassing, wasn't it? Mind you, we did laugh after you'd flounced out. I expect you did too.

He laughs. Rosie laughs, too, in spite of herself

Rosie As your income's now dropped so much, perhaps you'd better shove her off your desk, sit down at it, and earn some money.
Piers I'd like you both to meet. Shall I bring her up sometime?
Rosie You mean all over the carpet like yesterday's Tandoori?
Piers Really, Rosie. To be friends.
Rosie Ah, of course, friends. Why didn't I think of that? We can do lunch and discuss the menopause. She'll have to face it within the next thirty years.

Piers, while laughing at Rosie, quite enjoying her, is still, most determinedly, ploughing his own furrow. Rosie meanwhile, has warmed considerably, genuinely amused by Piers

Piers Oh, I do love you, Rosie. See? There is life after death for us. What fun you are.
Rosie Was she all on her own, this girl? Didn't she have a family or feller or husband or anything?
Piers Oh, there was a husband, yes.
Rosie Wow.
Piers An immature error on her part. She booted him out.
Rosie Did she really, the sweet old-fashioned thing?
Piers He's a sort of criminal, really.
Rosie Criminal?
Piers Ye-es. He's been to Borstal, or whatever they call it now, then done some real time.
Rosie In jail? What did he do?
Piers Oh, I don't know. Does it matter?
Rosie No, no.
Piers He's nothing but trouble. It was only Larissa kept him straight, apparently. She got a bit tired of the effort.
Rosie Poor thing.
Piers Ye-es, well, the point is … she's pregnant.
Rosie Pregnant?
Piers Yes.
Rosie By you?
Piers Of course by me, what do you think?

This hits Rosie, more than she realizes at first

Rosie So you're all right. I mean, not …
Piers Infertile?
Rosie Yes.
Piers No.
Rosie Well, well, well. So it was me, all that time.
Piers Looks like it.
Rosie What a way to find out. You poor old thing.
Piers No, no, we're delighted. It's — it's wonderful.

There is a crash and what could be a groan from the bedroom

    Whatever's that?
Rosie How should I know?

Piers Is someone in there?
Rosie Go and find out. It's your Home. Protect it.

Piers nervously goes to the bedroom door then backs off a little

Piers All right. Come out. We know you're in there.

No answer. Piers arms himself, opens the door and edges into the bedroom

   Oi. Come on. Out. You.
Rosie Behind the door, Piers. That's where they always are in films.

Piers jumps smartly back and peers through the crack

Piers No one there.
Rosie Or over your head, I saw in one picture.

Piers twists and cranes to peer anxiously up, then exits

Piers (*off*) I don't think there's — Hey, the window's open.
Rosie I opened that earlier. To give the room an airing.
Piers (*off*) He's got away. I'll call the police.
Rosie No, no, it must've been a cat or bird. Or the wind blew something over.

Piers enters

Piers Don't you want me to call the police?
Rosie We'd just look silly.
Piers What's going on, Rosie?
Rosie You tell me.
Piers The security chain on the door, now you're quite relaxed about intruders.
Rosie Why don't you bring her here?
Piers What?
Rosie Larissa. You wanted us to meet.
Piers Nothing's right about you today. What is it?
Rosie How about tomorrow?
Piers I want to talk to you first about money. Where we live. Who gets what.
Rosie No.
Piers You won't talk?

Rosie When I've met her: mum-to-be. That changes everything. Then I'll know how I feel.

Piers How you feel isn't relevant to the financial arithmetic ——

Rosie Oh, yes it is.

Piers —which is bloody. Things are really tight, Rosie. I've got all the figures from Maurice with me.

Rosie Ah, yes, Maurice, the Ken Dodd of creative accounting. [Ah, yes, Maurice, the man who turns drab, fiscal clay into Gothic horror for the Revenue.]

Piers You can get them checked by whoever you choose.

Rosie D'you really want this child or do you wish to hell you could get out of it all?

Piers Rosie, I can't let this go, I want it. I think it's because you and I couldn't — that's why we drifted apart.

Rosie And Larissa? Will she be satisfied with one?

Piers She says she's feeling very fertile. She wants four.

Rosie That's not fertility, that's incontinence. OK. Bring her. Goodbye.

Piers, wrongfooted, still feels something is wrong

Piers Right. Tomorrow about five, then.

Rosie Yes.

Piers But any nonsense and we're off. At once. Right?

Rosie You make it sound as though *I* suggested this meeting. You did.

Piers Yes. Right. Bye.

Rosie }
Piers } Bye.

And, with a last frustrated, suspicious glance round, Piers exits

Rosie hurries to put the chain on

Darren enters, wheezing

Rosie Where on earth did you hide?

Darren Behind that pile of junk under the bed. It's set off my asthma.

Rosie Wouldn't it just.

Darren Don't you ever dust in there?

Rosie Not with any passion.

Darren Pregnant. By Ferret Face. She'll have a litter. (*Big wheeze*) Oh, I haven't got my puffer with me.

Rosie (*confused*) Your puffer?

He gestures squeezing one down his throat

Darren It's in my saddlebag.
Rosie Oh, your inhaler. I thought you meant (*she gestures a train*) choo-choo. I'm going ga-ga. Shall I open a window?
Darren I have to relax.
Rosie Perhaps a drink would help.
Darren Herb tea?
Rosie Any particular sort?
Darren Whatever. But the water just below boiling, otherwise you de-oxygenate it.
Rosie God forbid we should do that.

She moves in and out of the kitchen, making the tea

Darren relaxes

Darren She wants *four*. I'll be a laughing stock: the man whose wife's got pregnant by a wrinkly.
Rosie How do you know it was Piers?
Darren (*shocked*) There's someone else too as well?
Rosie Well, how about *you*? You *are* married to her.
Darren Oh. Yes. No. We always practised safe sex. She insisted.
Rosie Did she?
Darren We were gonna plan our family. No having kids then breaking up, I couldn't handle that. I never seen my dad. I dunno who he is. Is he a bastard? I dunno, but I'm not. I wouldn't do that to my kids. Never. I'll be there when they want me. Always.
Rosie Are you really a criminal?

Darren does not answer

Safe sex, night school, loving father. You're the most uncriminal criminal.
Darren Listen to yourself. You'd rather joke than feel. That's why you'll lose this battle with them. You'll be too uptight to get stuck into the one thing that really matters.
Rosie What's that?
Darren Revenge. It's him you wanna screw.
Rosie Whatever for?
Darren You want this place, your jobs, money.
Rosie That's not revenge, that's justice.
Darren What are you like when you drop all that educated crap?
Rosie Like?
Darren Underneath.

Rosie Aaah. "Underneath you're a warm, real human being." (*Angrily*) There is no underneath. This is it.

Darren You know, your fuse is too short. If you cared about things it would grow longer.

Rosie Like Pinocchio's nose? I care, whoops. (*She gestures her nose growing*) I love you, whoops. (*Same again. She lets her rage run*) I have just blown most of my adult life on a man who for some time now — I'm not even sure how long — has just been a habit, like breakfast. I've been dumped by a packet of cornflakes. And, d'you know, faced with life without him, I've experienced panic, almost terror. I'm scared of being alone. Alone? I've been alone for years. The jokes as you call them — are the waste products of an under-used, neglected mind. It's had too little to do for twenty-odd years and it's discharging superfluous pollutants into the environment. I am a health hazard; an infectious, poisonous, out-dated, rusty piece of equipment whose only product is bile, the slurry of my so-called wit.

Pause

Darren I think your opinion of yourself is too low.

Rosie groans

(*Irritated*) Now what have I said? Don't tell me, I know: I've missed the point.

Rosie No. You have struck it on the head with a force that takes you beyond tautology into another dimension.

Darren I don't know what you're talking about.

Rosie My opinion of myself — and everything else — isn't nearly low enough.

Darren What about your jobs? Aren't they great? Doing good? Saving people and the environment and that?

Rosie You express it so eloquently.

Darren Oh, bollocks.

Rosie (*all just pouring out of her*) Everything's too late. Everything. This beautiful world, the blue planet, is being destroyed, all round us: the animals, the fish, the birds, the land, the seas, the rivers, the forests, even the air we breathe, or try to. Torturers aren't the most malignant pestilence on earth, *we* are the problem, all of us. There's a world-wide plague and we are it. There are six billion of us. We've done nothing but kill each other throughout history and there are still six *billion* of us. How ever many would there be if peace broke out? Oh, there's nothing in the situation that couldn't be saved by about five billion voluntary suicides but that seems unlikely, don't you think?

Darren You want to kill five billion people?

Rosie No, no, no, no, no. I don't want to kill anyone. Of course, what I should really do if I care about all this is to set an example and kill *myself*. But my suicide would only mean more destruction. There would be resources wasted on the inquest, then thousands of thermal units used to cremate me, or space wasted to bury me six feet down, too deep to provide nourishment for the plants. If I went to sea and threw myself overboard for the fishes, they'd send out search parties, wasting even more resources. If I stay alive I'm an ecological disaster, if I kill myself I'm a catastrophe.

Pause

Darren Is all that because he told you he was going to be a father?

Rosie I thought I'd come to terms with it. Piers and I rationalized the situation together: how wonderful, how responsible. No fertility clinics for us; not childless, we decided, but child-free. But privately each thought it was the other who was ... (*she finally brings herself to say it*) sterile. I've just been pleading for sterility from the whole human race and when I learn it's only me who can't ... (*she can't go on for a moment*) what a useless object I am.

Pause

Darren Would you like — would you like me to — um — give you a massage.

Rosie What?

Darren I'm very good at feet. Then I work upwards.

Rosie You mean you'll shag me?

Darren Well, if things develop.

Rosie Whatever for?

Darren I thought it might cheer you up a bit.

Rosie Of all the arrogant — to imagine that one dose of stiff dick would make the torture chambers disappear and streams sparkle over lichen-covered rocks. What a — I mean, how ... ? I'm speechless.

Darren If only you were. I was going to say that him — Ferret Face — telling you about them having a — he was the corkscrew who let the — um (*he gestures pulling a cork*) thingummy out of the whatsit.

Rosie A beautiful image.

Darren I was gonna say that he was the corkscrew and I was offering myself as the real screw, so to say.

They both stare at each other for a moment

Rosie Great balls of fire. What's this I hear? Word play?

Darren (*laughing, delighted*) Good, wannit? I thought of it as I said it. I was going to say corkscrew anyway, then I ——

Rosie Stop, stop, don't explain. (*She smiles at him, at her sweetest*) Let the process of your creativity be your own private mystery.

Darren Right. Yeah. Sorry. Well, d'you wanna give it a whirl?

He grins, but nervously, as Rosie considers him speculatively

I mean, I think I could handle it — I mean you. I mean it.

Rosie That is the most beguiling invitation I have ever had.

Darren Is humiliation part of your foreplay?

Rosie (*laughing*) Is this foreplay?

Darren gathers up his courage, goes to her and kisses her hand, all from a film. She is simply acquiescent. Encouraged, he kisses her up her arm, more warmly, puts an arm round her and starts to lead her towards the bedroom

(*Stopping*) Where do you think you're off to?

Darren Now who's asking obvious questions?

Rosie Because I let you kiss a bit of flesh, that's it, eh? Off we go, weh-hey. Why do you even want to bother to try?

Darren cannot answer that. He just stands, looking sheepish

It can't be because of — well — conventional lust.

Silence

Is it because I'm — well — unusual?

Silence

To you, anyway.

Silence

The conquest of the unknown?

Darren I've — sort of — got to like you.

Rosie Overcome by me, are you, poor thing?

Darren Well, not totally, no, but …

Rosie Oh, come on, don't be so coy.

Darren shrugs, embarrassed

Darren It's too rude to say.
Rosie Do you mean rude, impolite, or rude, filthy.
Darren Impolite. (*Earnestly*) Oh, I can be filthy too, if you want.
Rosie No, no, no. Just tell me. Sod the rudeness.
Darren I felt sorry for you.

Rosie stares

 And ...
Rosie Yes?
Darren I need somewhere to stay the night.
Rosie (*letting out a great gasp*) Ah. At last. We get to it. I'm a stopover for a — a — messenger boy ... who feels sorry for me.

And she laughs. He laughs too, relieved that she has taken it so well. He wipes imaginary sweat from his forehead. But to his horror her laugh changes into sobs where she has been heading for some while. Darren, shocked, goes to her

Darren I'm sorry. Sorry. I wouldn't have — you made me say it.

He goes to comfort her. But she suddenly lashes out at him

Rosie Get away. Get off me. Get away. Don't touch me.

And he is forced to retreat where he stands, breathing heavily, shocked and confused. This is all beyond him

Darren All right, all right, I was only ... Have your sodding breakdown on your own. I don't care.
Rosie (*pointing*) There, there.
Darren *What?* What d'you ——— ?
Rosie The spare-bloody-room, you oaf. If that's what you want.
Darren Oh.
Rosie Just leave me alone.

Black-out

SCENE 2

The same. The next afternoon

Darren is having a T'ai Chi session. He does this seriously and with utter concentration. His movements are not ungraceful

A key turns in the lock. The door is pushed open and Rosie enters. She is surprised to see Darren

Rosie How did you get in?

Darren points at the front door as part of one of his movements

How did you open it?

He points to the keys on a coffee table. She picks them up

Did you steal these?

Darren I had them made.

Rosie But how — oh, for Christ's sake stop that bloody nonsense and pay attention.

Darren (*without stopping*) From a set of your old man's.

Rosie I'll hit you if you don't …

And she physically impedes his movement. He stands still

Right. From the beginning: I gave you breakfast this morning, showed you out and double-locked the door. You got on your bike and rode off into the sunrise; I went to work. When I come back you're in here again. How?

She exits to the bedroom, glancing at her watch

Darren The first day Ferret Face moved in with Rissa, before they changed the locks, I went back home while they were at work — just to see. You know. He'd left these keys by the bed. I had 'em copied — just in case. Then I came round here when you were at work and tried 'em out — just to see. Then I used to come regular.

Rosie enters with hairbrush and make-up, shocked by his words. Throughout the following she prepares herself for the imminent meeting

I been in your flat loads o' times before I met you yesterday. You got nothing to be afraid of. I just wanted to see.

Rosie (*not at all pleased*) You've been coming in here ...?
Darren I always thought he'd have some old dog of a wife. But you ... I
came here a few times just to sit here. To think. 'S nice, innit? Elegant.

Rosie does not feel at all secure, a condition she does not care for

Rosie What were the crimes you committed that got you into trouble?
Darren (*shrugging*) I wanna look forward, not back.
Rosie *What did you do?*
Darren Only twocking.
Rosie What?
Darren Twocking.
Rosie What on earth is that?
Darren Nicking cars, Taking Without Owner's Consent, joy-riding.
Rosie Is that all?
Darren Yes.
Rosie But you went to prison. (*She realizes*) You crashed into someone,
a pedestrian or someone.
Darren No, no, no. My mate, Shaun. He was in the car with me. We
turned it over.
Rosie *We* turned it over. You couldn't both have been driving.
Darren Him. Me. I dunno. We was well pissed. What's the difference?
Rosie Rather a lot, I should have thought.
Darren He's still dead. I knocked it on the head after that.
Rosie Hm. (*Gently*) Anyway, I'm afraid you still have to go.
Darren What about Rissa and Ferret Face? Don't you want me here for
when they come?
Rosie I don't see what good'll come of a mass confrontation.

He climbs over the back of the sofa, crowding her

Darren Ah, go on. Be fun. Getting one over on them two.
Rosie You're too ... unpredictable for my taste. (*She moves quickly
away*)
Darren No fun if you know what people are gonna do.

The doorbell rings, the same idiosyncratic ring as in Scene 1

Rosie It's them.
Darren I'll hide again.
Rosie No.
Darren Bring the conversation round to her being in the club, then I'll
come in.

Rosie Oh. Oh, all right. To hell with 'em. But leave enough time for me to get a good look at her.
Darren Right.

Darren goes into the bedroom

A key is put in the lock, the door is opened. Piers ushers in Larissa

Piers Ah, no chain on today. Well, here we are.
Larissa Oh, it's lovely.
Piers Ah! Rosie. There you are again.
Rosie So I am again.
Piers Yes. Larissa this is Rosie, my — um ...
Rosie Wife.
Piers Quite. And Rosie this is Larissa, my — um ...
Rosie Bit on the side.
Piers Thank you, Rosie. Secretary. (*To Larissa*) I warned you.
Larissa It's all right. Relax, Weetie. (*And she pats him*)
Rosie Oh, no, no, sorry. You're not on the side any more, are you?
Larissa Not really, no.
Rosie More on your back now. How d'you do.
Piers Rosie.
Larissa Pleased to meet you.

Rosie tries to look at Larissa upside down

Rosie Yes, yes. I'd know you anywhere now that I can see you properly.
Piers *Rosie!*
Larissa Oh, don't. I could have died. Like a *Carry On* film, wasn't it?
Rosie Not very.
Larissa You look much less frightening this way up.
Rosie So do you.
Larissa Anyway, I'm glad to meet you on level terms, so to speak, sort of thing.
Piers Oh, yes, very good, darling. (*He laughs*)
Rosie Well, now, what can I offer you, Mrs Tucker? Tea, coffee, a drink?
Larissa Oh, no. No alcohol, thank you.
Piers You know her name.
Rosie (*caught*) No, just guessed. Amazing, aren't I?
Larissa D'you have any 'erb tea, please? Or just hot water with a squidge of lemon?

Rosie Either.

Larissa 'Erb tea, please.

Piers You can't just have guessed.

Rosie Oh yes I can. Any particular 'erb?

Larissa Er — no. Whatever is great.

Rosie And don't boil the water or else you de-oxygenate it.

Larissa (*surprised and pleased*) That's right. Great minds think alike.

Piers But I'm sure I've not mentioned her name, her surname. I always called her Larissa.

Rosie No, no, don't you remember? You had a little rhyme about her. "My P.A.'s name is Tucker. Oh, how I love to ..."

Rosie exits quickly to the kitchen

Piers I'm sure I never ——

Larissa Does it matter, Weetie?

Piers Ssh. Try not to call me Weetie. It'll only ——

Larissa Oh, poo. Sorry. I'll try to remember.

Piers I told you. Any excuse and she's in there.

Larissa Relax, Wee — relax. I can handle it. It's you that's worrying. Just relax.

Piers I know her.

Larissa And I will, too, if you just give us a chance.

Rosie returns, with a tray of tea things

I love your flat. So nice and airy. Spacious.

Rosie Yes.

Larissa Better than my rabbit hutch.

Rosie Piers said it was very cosy. And convenient.

Larissa Convenient?

Rosie For the M25. Exit 24, isn't it?

Larissa Oh, yeah. Since Piers moved in, if he gets out of order, I call him The Potters Bar Turn-Off. (*She laughs*) That stops him.

Rosie is surprised at this

Rosie Well. That's very — well done, Mrs Tucker.

Larissa Please call me Larissa, would you?

Rosie Right. And you'd better call me Rosie or else we'll both be calling each other Mrs Boston soon, won't we? Marks one and two.

Rosie exits to the kitchen

Larissa (*laughing*) Oh, dear, yes. I hadn't thought of that. Oh, dear. Isn't it awful? I'm ever so sorry.

Rosie returns with a pot of tea

Rosie Please — you mustn't torture yourself.

Larissa You're terrible, aren't you? You never let up. Weetie said you wouldn't.

Rosie What?

Larissa He said you'd only have to hear the way I speak and you'd start putting the boot in.

Rosie No, no, what did you call him?

Larissa Oh, blow, I said I wouldn't. Sorry, Weetie.

Rosie (*giving Larissa tea*) Weetie. As in Sweetie without the S?

Larissa (*pleased*) Yes. You got it at once. Not everyone does.

Piers It's just a pet name, Rosie.

Rosie (*passing him a cup*) Weetie.

Larissa And I want you to know that I don't have designs on your home. Really. I know Weetie wants us to move in here just for a while, for convenience, and I think that's reasonable.

Rosie Do you?

Larissa But I want us to have our own place. New. Our own fresh start.

Rosie Ah?

Larissa Yes. And I want you to know that I don't bear you any malice at all. And I don't think you should me.

Rosie Don't you?

Larissa No, because after the shock and the changeover is done, I haven't stolen anything from you, have I? Weetie's told me. You've gone your own way for yonks and yonks now and you're much more taken up with your jobs than him, and Weetie and me have found each other, and when you're free you'll find someone too, you're not that old. And everybody can be happy ever after.

Pause

Rosie What about your husband?

Larissa He'll get over it. He's young. That's it really. He's too young for me. Immature, really.

Rosie Yes.

Larissa He'll find his life's partner when he grows up, and Weetie's just right for me. He loves my little ways and I feel safe with him. Protected. I'm happy. For the first time. I can flower, properly.

Piers She's wonderful, isn't she?

Rosie She's a dinosaur. You've paired off with a dinosaur in high heels and costume jewellery. She's officially extinct.

Piers The thing about Larissa is, she's not ashamed to show her feelings. It's charming but very vulnerable. I'm not used to it. Not yet. But I'm making the journey.

Rosie Ah, yes. That universal journey.

Larissa I'll say he is. You should hear what Piers calls me ——

Piers — not now, darling ——

Larissa — when he's not feeling shy in front of you. And everyone has pet names for their children when they're little, don't they?

Rosie Do they?

Larissa Oh, sorry, sorry, I forgot. (*Did she?*) You don't have any, do you? I'm really sorry.

Rosie Nothing to be sorry about.

Larissa Oh, well, that's fine, then.

Piers Larissa has a pet, you know: a lovely Blue Persian kitten.

Larissa Oh, yes. He gave it to me. He's lovely, just — wooh — I call him Fluffy.

Rosie Oh, really? Why's that?

Larissa Well, because he's ——

Piers (*quickly*) Don't answer her, darling.

Larissa Eh? Oh.

Rosie So you think pet names are the answer, eh? The way to save all those foundering marriages?

Larissa No, I think they're the outward and visible sign of an inward and spiritual love. And you shouldn't bottle it up.

Rosie lets all this sink in

Rosie Piers, you poor deprived Weetie. I'd like to apologize for my shortcomings. (*She pauses briefly*) Now what's your pet name for her? I'm dying to know.

Piers Nothing.

Rosie Ooh.

Piers You only——

Larissa Goddy.

A brief pause

Rosie Sorry?

Larissa Goddy.

Rosie Ah.

Larissa It's short for something.

Rosie Wait a minute. Don't tell me ... Godzilla.
Piers ⎫ (*together*) ⎧Oh, no. You shouldn't ever give her a chance to ——
Larissa ⎭   ⎩That's exactly what *I* said. Great minds think alike.
Rosie Godawful? Godhelpus? Godalmighty?

*Between each of Rosie's suggestions Larissa shakes her head, giggling,
pleased to join in the game, taking no offence*

Larissa No-o-o ... (*Proudly*) Goddess.
Rosie (*floored*) Oh, yes, of course. I should have got that. Silly of me.
Larissa No-one's ever called me that before.
Rosie No, no ... no. Nor me either.

Darren appears at the bedroom door

*Larissa sees him first and lets out a squawk of dismay and astonishment.
Piers sees Darren and jumps out of his skin*

Piers Who the hell are you?

*Things move very fast from here, with the two separate conversations
overlapping. Darren increasingly overplays the injured husband role*

Rosie This is Darren, darling, a new friend of mine. (*To Larissa*) I
believe you know your husband already.
Piers Are you her ... ? (*To Larissa*) Is he your ... ?
Darren (*to Larissa*) Traitor.
Piers What's going on here?
Darren Weetie. How could you?
Larissa It's all over, Daz. You have to accept that.
Piers Was he that noise in the other room yesterday?
Darren But Weetie, *him*, Ferret Face.
Larissa You're just using him to focus your heartache.
Darren I'm talking about you calling him Weetie.
Piers (*to Larissa*) You don't have to put up with this. We're going.
Really, Rosie. To subject a pregnant woman to this.
Rosie She's only a little bit pregnant. She can still stand up for a month
or two.
Darren (*wildly*) Pregnant? Pregnant? Did you say she's ...? Are
you ...?
Larissa Yes. So grow up.
Darren By him? By that old porker? You'll have a piglet. (*And he reels
away in agony up to the wall*)

Rosie *(to Darren)* All right. Take it easy.

Piers God, what a lout.

Darren He'll be so ancient when it's grown up you'll be able to have a combined twenty-first and embalming ceremony.

Larissa Maybe we should go, Weetie.

Darren *(shouting)* Don't call him that. I can't stand it.

Larissa Weetie, Weetie, Weetie.

Darren *(distraught, to Rosie)* That was her name for me.

Rosie Weetie?

Darren Yes.

Piers *(to Larissa)* Is that true?

Larissa We-ell.

Darren Our special name.

Piers No, it's not. It's ours.

Rosie Not very inventive, is she?

Darren Traitor. *(He grabs one of the two Turners from its place on the wall)*

Piers I don't think I'll ever forgive you for this, Rosie.

Rosie I didn't ask you to bring her here.

Piers Yes, you did. You invited her yesterday.

Rosie Oh, yes. So I did. Well, I didn't invite him. He just ——

At this point Darren brings the painting crashing down over Pier's head and shoulders. The painting tears apart. Piers yells out and ends up with the frame pinning his arms to his sides, elbows bent, his hands up, trapped in the painting. He is shocked and frightened, but not hurt. Larissa screams as Darren goes for the other painting as Rosie gasps in shock and dismay

Larissa Weetie. Weetie. Are you all right?

Piers turns and sees the gap on the wall

Piers It's the Turner. It's one of the Turners. He's mad. He's — Look out, darling.

But too late. Darren has brought the other one crashing down over Larissa's head with the same result. Larissa screams. Rosie screams too

Aah. That's the other one. That's two million. He's just destroyed over two million pounds. He's insane. Criminally ——

Darren *(shouting at Piers)* Stick it up your arse, Grandad.

Larissa *(sobbing)* I can't move. My nose hurts. He's cut my nose off.

Darren It stuck out too much, anyway.

Rosie helps Piers out of his frame

Larissa I'm bleeding. I'm bleeding.
Piers Get me out of here. I want the police.
Rosie Stand still.
Piers They've been in my family for generations.
Larissa Oh, help me, someone. Help me.
Rosie There.
Piers You bloody vandal. I'll kill you.

Darren dives over the sofa and hides behind the furniture, Rosie and Larissa. Piers sets off after him

Darren You'll go to gaol.
Piers So will you, via the bloody hospital. You pea-brained, clod-hopping, destructive savage.
Darren Oh, you're like a rutting stag.

Piers lunges at Darren who avoids him as Piers crashes fruitlessly and painfully into something

(*Taunting him*) Nearly, nearly.
Rosie Don't be silly, Piers. Call the police.
Piers Call the police. Go on. Call 'em.
Rosie I just said that.
Larissa Please. *Please*. Somebody help me.
Piers It's a nightmare. (*He picks up phone and dials*)
Rosie Oh, shut up. You're all right.
Larissa Weetie, please. Help me.
Rosie What are the police going to do? Stick 'em back together again?
Piers I'll see him in gaol though.

Darren suddenly seems to find an unusual amount of authority

Darren Oh no you won't. She's my wife, you've got her pregnant, I just found out. It's a crime of passion. No jury will convict me.

Piers stops dead; Darren has a point

Yeah. See? How would you feel if I told you I'd got her (*indicating Rosie*) pregnant?

Piers Don't be disgusting. (*He bangs the phone down*)
Rosie Oh, lovely. Thank you.
Piers (*to Rosie*) Have you been — with him?
Rosie Oh, don't be so daft. Get the police.
Piers I don't believe it.
Larissa (*sobbing*) I want to go home. Please, Weetie.
Darren Oh, shut up.

Larissa manages to stick two fingers up at him, her hand just above the painting

Rosie Anyway, what's disgusting about him and me, any more than you two?

Piers takes the painting off Larissa, giving her another shock and making her squawk again

Piers Are you all right, darling? This is awful. My Turners … He's a savage.
Rosie Piers, I'm talking to you. What's disgusting about —— ?
Larissa Weetie, I'm going. This minute. Are you coming? (*To Darren*) You're vile. I hate you. (*She hits him with her handbag*) You're *worse* than a murderer this time. You'll go to jail for ever.

Larissa runs out

Piers No, Goddy. Wait. I'm … (*He stops and looks at Rosie and Darren*) You, him, this.
Larissa (*off, very loudly*) Weetie.
Piers It's not fair, Rosie. It's just not fair.

Piers goes reluctantly

Darren Wicked. Put the chain on.
Rosie What d'you mean put the chain on? You get out first.

Darren puts the chain on the door

Darren I don't want them coming back. (*Quite suddenly, he is utterly calm, in charge of himself*)
Rosie (*a bit frightened*) What are you going to do now?

Darren disappears into the bedroom

(*Picking up one of the ripped paintings, near to tears*) I can't believe
... (*She trails off*)

*Darren enters carrying the two unframed Turners, one in each hand,
he sets them down, on display*

Rosie looks from them to the torn, framed one she is holding

What?
Darren (*taking her painting*) Photocopy. From the lab where I'm
messenger. Beautiful quality they get, don't they?

Rosie can't take it in

Took the paintings down there this morning. Hundred-per-cent-accurate
laser reproductions, stick 'em on distressed canvas. Whack them two
over the head and you're the proud owner of two Turners worth a
million pounds each. There.
Rosie But that's robbery, stealing or something.
Darren You can't steal from your husband. What's his is yours in law.
And when you're divorced what's yours'll be your own.

*He takes full charge of events and, increasingly throughout the scene, of
Rosie, something she finds she enjoys*

Rosie But he'll claim the insurance.
Darren Let him.
Rosie But that'll be fraud.
Darren Ye-ah. Hope he doesn't get caught.
Rosie But I'll be an accessory or something.
Darren You're not responsible for his deranged actions.
Rosie But it's dishonest.
Darren Oh, dear.
Rosie But *you're* liable. *You* destroyed them. The insurance
company'll ——
Darren My Lord, faced with the disgusting, degrading taunt that this
man, old enough to be my father, had impregnated my lovely young
wife, My Lord, I don't know what came over me. There was a red mist
and the next thing I knew the two of them were framed. Yes, yes, poor
boy. Two years' probation.

Rosie laughs, in spite of her reservations, but she is far from reassured

Rosie Will they pay up? The insurance?

Darren If they don't, you've got the paintings. If they do, you've got the paintings *and* your share of the insurance payout in the divorce settlement.

Rosie But what shall I do with 'em?

Darren Stick 'em on the wall?

Rosie This is all too easy. There must be a catch.

Darren They're not stolen. They don't exist. Of course, we'll have to hide 'em for a bit. Somewhere brilliant.

Rosie is becoming increasingly torn between amused admiration for Darren and ingrained antipathy for the gimcrack situation he has created

Rosie How do you know all the details, the …?

Darren I shared a cell with a forger.

Darren is on a high, pleased with his own cleverness, but even more delighted whenever Rosie shows any sign of amusement or approval

Rosie You'll get caught again.

Darren Only *you* know. You're not going to shop me, are you?

Rosie is appalled to be put on the spot like that

Rosie Oh, now, don't involve me in your …

Darren exits to the kitchen. He immediately returns with a black bag, scissors and Stanley knife

Yes.

Darren You're not going to shop me, are you?

Rosie The insurance'll want to see the remains.

Darren I destroyed them in terror, My Lord. I see now that was foolish, but in my passion …

Rosie Was all this for me?

Darren gives a great, big insincere grin, intended to disarm

Darren Yeah. Course it was. I think you're great.

Rosie You liar. (*She laughs*) You lovely liar.

Rosie would like to throw her arms round him, but doesn't. They are both laughing or half-laughing with each other

Darren Are you on for it?

Rosie nods, excited

Rosie I suppose we can always find them again. Say it was some sort of mistake.
Darren Right on.
Rosie Meanwhile, we can torment Piers like ... (*She laughs again*)
Darren Revenge, see? Power. Greatest emotion known to man.
Rosie I'd forgotten what fun things could — just fun, *fun*. (*She laughs wildly and perhaps does a little dance*) Is that what revenge does for you?
Darren No. (*He kisses her quickly*) That's animal magnetism.

Darren tries to kiss her properly

Rosie Hey, cut it out.
Darren Rosie, I got something else to tell you.
Rosie What?
Darren I love you.
Rosie Don't be so bloody silly.
Darren No, no, no, I do. Listen. I know everything about you.
Rosie What?
Darren When I came in here, without permission, I searched the whole place. And — well — I found — d'you know what I found?
Rosie What?
Darren *You*. Everywhere. I found your letters, your papers, your make-up, your ... I found, well, your mind, I suppose.
Rosie You've read my letters?
Darren I've seen everything that's in here. I know everything you wear. I even know what sort of undies you — they're lovely. Like you. I put 'em on.

Rosie is, of course, disturbed. Darren thinks he has been clever. He has no thought that she might be anything other than pleased

Rosie You've put my knickers on?
Darren I just wanted to — be close to you. I just sank myself into you. You're ... well, you. You really get to me.
Rosie Do I?

Darren Yeah.

A moment

> First, we hide these (*indicating the paintings*) Then we take this
> (*indicating the black bag*) down to the river, a bridge'll be best. In the
> middle. We cut them up into half-inch squares and watch them float out
> on the tide. (*He gestures expansively*)
> **Rosie** You *have* thought of everything. Where are we going to hide
> these?

Darren taps the side of his nose, laughing

Darren Don't you worry. No-one'll ever find 'em.
Rosie Then?
Darren Then we come back here and — whatever you say.
Rosie No.
Darren What?
Rosie That's what I say: no.
Darren (*confidently*) OK, you're the boss.
Rosie Am I? So I am.

And he turns to one of the paintings

Darren (*triumphantly*) See? Revenge.

*Perhaps he holds it up. Rosie (or Darren) grabs the other framed fake
and holds it aloft in triumph*

Rosie or Darren The revenge of the dumpees.

And they laugh as ——

—— the CURTAIN *falls*

ACT II
SCENE 1

The same. Early evening the following May

There are examples of Larissa's possessions and taste around the flat, including, possibly, replacement paintings

The heavily pregnant Larissa is laying the table for four. She is taking care but is in a lacklustre mood. She stops for a moment and holds her pregnancy in both hands

Larissa No, no, *stop it*. Go to sleep. (*She stands for a moment longer, holding herself, until she is obeyed*) Good boy.

A key turns in the lock

   Piers enters, very end-of-day. Larissa is at once the cheerful little woman

   Hallo, Weetie.
Piers (*echoing her dully*) Hallo, Goddy. (*He picks up and looks at two letters but they are not for him*)
Larissa Come and say hallo to Bumpy.
Piers Hallo, Bumpy.
Larissa No, come and say hallo properly. *Feel* hallo.
Piers It's been a bitch of a day, dear.
Larissa (*holding herself*) Oo, Bumpy's waving hallo to Daddy. Look. Feel. He's had a tricky day, too. He's been thumping about in there. We'll have to call him that: thumpy. Thumpy's been feeling a bit grumpy.
Piers No-one can hear you, can they?
Larissa Course not. Come on, Daddy. Bonding time. Bond with Bumpy.

Piers kneels in front of her

   There. Feel?

Piers feels

   Wave.

Piers waves weakly

Wave, hallo, Daddy, I'm so happy to feel you feeling me. Say hallo,
Bumpy.
Piers Hallo, Bumpy.
Larissa And Daddy's happy to see you, too, Bumpy.
Piers Look, dear, I don't think I'm up to this. (*And he goes and sits down
limply*)
Larissa Daddy's not himself tonight, Bumpy. (*She laughs*) He's feeling
a bit Humpy. You have a little zizz and I'll get Humpy a nice glass of
Scotch.
Piers I could murder a very large one, no water.

Larissa brings him a drink

Larissa (*to her bump*) No, no, this is not for you, it's for Daddy.
Piers What?
Larissa I was talking to Bumpy.
Piers Oh, yes.

She gives him his drink

Larissa Now tell us all about it. Bumpy's longing to hear. He's so
excited he's quite jumpy. Did you get any money?
Piers The Department of Social Security say I don't qualify for the
dole.
Larissa Oh, dear.
Piers They say I'm not unemployed. What the bloody hell do they think
I am? My business goes bust; I can't earn any money; no-one'll give a
job to a man who's over — my age.
Larissa Fifty-three, Weetie. And we love every minute of you.
Piers They say, you can't be unemployed if you were self-employed.
They say I have to apply for income support. Only I don't qualify
for that either, according to their rulebook, which seems to have been
drawn up by the Spanish Inquisition. Income *support*? I haven't got
any income to support.
Larissa Why don't we qualify, Weetie?
Piers Principally because I wore a suit, spoke English and didn't sport a
nose ring. Bloody welfare state, they pay out to every Tom, Dick and
Abdul for decades when I'm working, then stop when I'm not.
Larissa What about the insurance company?
Piers Ah, them. They've finally made up their mind.
Larissa Yes?

Piers They won't pay out a penny without the evidence of the destroyed paintings.

Larissa Oh, no.

Piers They say I've got to sue them for it to indemnify them. Only I can't because I've got no money. So I went to the legal-aid people. Guess what? I don't qualify for legal aid. And on top of that the police won't charge that bastard husband of yours, they call it a domestic. Two million pounds worth of domesticity. So *I've* got to sue him. Only I can't because I've got no money and even if I won he's got nothing for me to get off him. So, all in all, I think we're up what is commonly known in nautical circles as shit creek.

Larissa You'll think of something, Weetie, I know you will.

Piers (*with a weary smile*) You're wonderful. Goddy by name and Goddy by nature.

Larissa Only try to think of it soon, Weetie. Bumpy's getting lumpier ever day. I'm going to go pop any minute now and we're going to disappear under a pile of nappies and poo.

Piers (*doing his best*) I can't wait, Goddy.

Larissa Don't be too sure.

And they embrace awkwardly as a key turns in the lock

Rosie enters. She is in an impenetrably good humour, almost on a high. She picks up and looks at the two letters before replacing them

Rosie Evening all. How are the lovebirds?

Piers Who have you been saving today: the oppressed or the planet?

Rosie Mondays and Tuesdays, the oppressed; Wednesdays and Thursdays, the planet.

Piers I suppose nobody paid you for your efforts.

Rosie Try not to be venal, Piers.

Larissa Bumpy wanted to know if Auntie Rosie got his prescription from the chemists.

Rosie She certainly did and I hope Bumpy's blooming — if that's the right word.

She takes a paper bag from her handbag and gives it to Larissa

(*Seeing the laid table*) Oh. Does that mean that food is happening?

Larissa Yes, 's all in the kitchen, ready.

Rosie What is it?

Larissa It says on the packets.

Rosie Only Darren and I might be going out to eat. If that's all right. A sort of celebration.

Rosie goes off to one of the bedrooms to deposit things

Piers How come she's got money to eat out?
Larissa (*going towards the kitchen*) I shouldn't have de-freezed them packets, Bumpy. You could get salmonella. And we don't want that, do we, before you've even popped out and said, "Hallo Mummy"?

Larissa goes as Rosie returns

Piers So what have you got to celebrate?
Rosie (*with a big smile*) My entire life.
Piers I went to see the insurance company today. They won't pay out.
Rosie The meanies.
Piers They want evidence that those paintings were actually destroyed.
Rosie Mistrustful meanies.
Piers They still want to interview you. You saw it all too.
Rosie If they won't believe you and Larissa I'm not getting involved.
Piers You *are* involved, bloody hell's teeth, what's the matter with you? If they pay up you can get rid of us from here, live your entire life with Young Buggerlugs and have plenty of money.
Rosie Money doesn't bring happiness, Piers. You should know that.
Piers Oh, shut up. You won't always be floating on a cloud of coitus ecstaticus.
Rosie It seems to be keeping me nicely airborne for the time being.
Piers I raised hell in that insurance office. I begged, I pleaded, I ranted, I raved.
Rosie I'm sorry I missed that.
Piers They're barely even polite any more.
Rosie I should sue if I were you. Hey, that rhymes. (*Singing*) I should sue, if I were you.
Piers Oh, God, don't *you* start.

Larissa enters

Rosie You know, you look really wonderful, Larissa. A picture.
Larissa Oh, don't. I look like a football with knobs on.
Rosie But a glowing, healthy, productive football.

There is a moment between them

Larissa Would you like to feel Bumpy? He likes it — people contacting him. Makes him feel wanted.
Rosie (*smiling*) How do you know?
Larissa I know everything about Bumpy. Go on.

After a moment's hesitation Rosie does so

Rosie Oh, well. Cheers.
Larissa There. See? Say hallo, Bumpy.
Rosie Hallo, Bumpy.
Larissa No, no, I mean Bumpy, say hallo to you.
Rosie Oh. Sorry ... Oh ... Oh ... Is that ... ? He's just ... I can ——
Larissa He's waving.
Rosie Yes ... It feels like a wave — a ripple almost — right across ... (*A sudden movement from inside*) Wow, that was ... May I?
Larissa What?

Rosie kneels down, puts her head against Larissa and listens

He can't talk yet, you know.
Rosie I can hear a sort of grumble.
Larissa That's me wanting my dinner. He kicks, he waves, he boxes and he tap dances, but he's not chatty Bumpy. A bit like his daddy, sometimes.

The front door opens and Darren enters

Rosie (*delighted*) He's doing it again. I think it's the tap dance this time. (*She laughs*) He's a whirling dervish. Hey, Darren. Here. Come and feel this. He can, can't he?
Darren No, thank you.

Darren picks up the two letters

Rosie But it's wonderful.
Darren Yeah. Fabulous. Get Porky to have a feel with his front trotter.
Piers The Oscar Wilde of the cycle lane is back.
Darren (*going off*) Oink, oink, oink, oink.

Darren exits

Piers You know all those motorists that keep missing you on that bike, they need arresting for careless driving. (*To Rosie and Larissa*) Don't look at me. It's always the same: a perfectly nice atmosphere in the place, then the winner of the Tour de Wapping comes in.

Piers exits huffily to another bedroom

Larissa All them animals in herds and flocks and things, they've got it right, haven't they?

Rosie You mean, only one male and all the rest female?

Rosie ⎫   *(together)* ⎧ Yes.
Larissa ⎭   ⎩ Yeah. I hope you're a girl, Bumpy. No problem.

Larissa exits to the kitchen as Darren enters. He stands and looks smugly at Rosie

Rosie Well?

He pauses momentarily

Darren Have a guess.
Rosie Oh, shut up.
Darren Yes.
Rosie Really?
Darren Yes.
Rosie Both?
Darren Yes. Both. *Yes.*

He throws his arms round her in enthusiasm. She breaks away

Rosie You've got the job? They've confirmed it in writing?
Darren Yes.
Rosie And what marks did you get in the paper?
Darren Well. (*He has two letters with which he fiddles*)
Rosie Show me, show me, show me. (*She practically snatches the two letters from him*)
Darren That one's about the diploma.
Rosie (*reading*) Theory: seventy-six …
Darren (*laughing*) Sorry, sorry.
Rosie Practical: *eighty-four.* You — you — a *distinction.*
Darren Just. Just, by that much —— (*He holds up finger and thumb, measuring a tiny gap*)
Rosie Doesn't matter by how much, that's equivalent to a First.
Darren — I squeaked it ——
Rosie Oh, Darren, Darren — (*she throws her arms round him and perhaps her legs, too*) — you clever old thing.
Darren No, no, you're the clever one.
Rosie We both are. Well done, well done, well done.
Darren YEE-EES.

He has her off the floor, whirling her round

Rosie We're going to eat out tonight. Somewhere wonderful. I'll write out a cheque that'll bounce all the way to the bank and back.

Darren (*pointing to the letter in her hand*) And *that* one's about the job.

Rosie (*glancing at it*) Trainee Junior Managerial Executive … (*She laughs*) What grisly jargon they do use. (*She hugs him*)

Darren You know — I feel — I …

Rosie Yes?

Darren The best I've ever felt in my whole life. And it's all because of you.

Rosie (*putting a hand on his mouth*) Ssh. Just be proud of yourself.

Darren You always know best.

Rosie Yes.

Another embrace

Darren OK, Teacher, I'll go and have a bath, then we can get going.

Rosie I'll come and give you a massage. In the bath.

Darren (*a grin*) Dirty cow.

Rosie Soap your back.

Darren OK.

Rosie And your front, too.

Darren All over. Come and get in with me.

Rosie Oh, all right, if you insist.

Another embrace

   Larissa enters

Rosie and Darren break and Darren makes to leave nearly bumping into Larissa

Darren Urgh.

Larissa Hey, watch it.

Darren Watch it? Waffor? Does it juggle? (*He sidles round her*)

Larissa Urgh to you too. (*Thrusting her pregnancy at him*) Urgh, urgh, urgh, urgh.

   Darren jumps back and exits chased by Larissa

Rosie is watching

   Larissa immediately returns

What's up?

Rosie No, no, nothing. It's just that — seeing you using your — erm — using Bumpy as a battering ram seems so — er ...

Larissa Don't worry. I knew Darren wouldn't touch me with a barge-pole. (*She picks up the letters and reads them*)

Rosie He doesn't seem to like pregnancy. Some men don't, I believe.

Larissa No, it's not that. It's me. I make him sick.

Rosie *You* do?

Larissa He can't handle knowing that Piers 'n' me — did this.

Rosie Ah.

Larissa It's a bummer, innit? Darren gets into the fast lane, Piers goes bust. I blow up like a balloon, you glow like an electric fire. We get evicted, you take us in.

Rosie You were homeless, we couldn't leave you on the streets.

Larissa I've never met a good person before, I mean a really good one. I mean in your personal life as well as your work.

Rosie Isn't one's work one's personal life?

Larissa One's work one's personal life. You don't know you're born, do you? Saving the world two days a week; getting people out of prison two days a week; three days left to shag Darren and think about it all.

Rosie Look, I've got to go.

Larissa Oh, yeah. Your bonk in the bath. He really does it for you, doesn't he?

Rosie (*changing tack*) Tell me something, something I don't understand: didn't you ever fancy Darren enough to ...?

Larissa Gobble him up. Like you do?

Rosie No, just to stay with him.

Larissa No.

Rosie Haven't you ever felt something like that — just a bit — about anyone?

Larissa No.

Rosie Not Piers?

Larissa laughs

What about on the desk in the office? All that?

Larissa (*pulling a face*) Oh, yeah, yeah.

Rosie (*stumped*) Oh.

Larissa I don't think I've ever felt like you do now. Or ever will.

Rosie Oh, you're wrong, you're — you can't tell. I thought I'd never... D'you know, I'd like to tear Darren into long thin strips and eat him. Slowly. Like spaghetti.

Larissa And out of bed?

Rosie Oh yes, mind and spirit. I just sing to be with him, and when he looks at me, the Hallelujah Chorus.

Larissa You really wanted to get all that off your chest to someone, didn't you?

Rosie I'm pregnant. I'm going to tell Darren in a minute. In the bath. (*She laughs in delight then catches herself*) Hah, I'm terrified he'll — but I'm laughing all the same. I don't know what to do with myself. I'm so happy, I feel like a girl, it's ridiculous, isn't it?

Larissa I thought you couldn't.

Rosie I thought I couldn't too. Piers'll be astonished.

Larissa Darren'll be a bit surprised too, won't he?

Rosie (*laughing*) I'm terrified to tell him. No, I'm not. I mean, I *should* be terrified but I'm not. I — I — I think I must be I *should* be ——

Larissa It's called hormones.

Rosie What?

Larissa Bloody nature. Pregnancy. Makes your brain go soft. You're baby-happy. Like me. You feel great when you should be shitting bricks. It's all hormones. Taking care of the next generation.

Pause

Rosie Promise me something?

Larissa What?

Rosie Keep quiet about it. For the moment. Perhaps I won't mention — this is *his* day.

Larissa Sure.

Rosie Thank you.

Larissa Rosie.

Rosie Yes.

Larissa All that wanting to tear him up and eat him like spaghetti — does he feel like that about you?

Rosie Yes. (*She thinks about it, then is less certain*) Yes. Of course he does.

Larissa That's all right, then.

Pause

Rosie What d'you mean?

Larissa We-ell. It's not what you feel about the bloke that matters, is it? It's what the bloke feels about you. Are you going to go with him?

Rosie What?

Larissa Darren. To Swindon.

Rosie Swindon? Whatever for.

Larissa holds out the letter. Rosie takes it

Larissa That's where he's going, innit?
Rosie (*reading*) I didn't — I didn't read that. I … (*She is stricken*) Darren
went for his interview here in London. He just showed me the letter.
Larissa Yeah. Well. That's Darren.

Rosie quickly goes, brushing past Piers who is entering

Piers Whoops. Pardon me for taking up all that space.
Larissa Nothing like a quick poke in the bath before supper, is there?
Piers My God, she's changed.

Larissa hands him the letter

Larissa They might be going to Swindon.
Piers Swindon? Rosie? Don't make me laugh. (*He laughs. Stopping
suddenly*) That means we get this place.

Black-out

Scene 2

The same. Later that evening

The room is in darkness except for the flickering TV

*Piers is alone, very drunk, surfing the TV with the remote control in his
hand. An RP voice from the set is putting a government gloss on the
employment situation in a smug way that infuriates Piers*

Television Voice Unemployment showed an increase last month contrary
to government predictions. There were three thousand more jobless
after the figures had been seasonally adjusted. A spokesperson for the
Department of Employment said this was just a blip in an otherwise
downward trend that had been evident for the last ——
Piers (*pressing the remote control; snarling*) Oh, sod off.

*There are sounds of approaching sexual climax between two Americans
from the television*

Female Voice Oh, God, Harvey, that's too — that's just — you can't —
Oh, no.

Male Voice Yes, Baby, I can. Yes, yes, yes, you want it.
Female Voice Oh, no, no, no, no, please.
Piers For God's sake give her one and we can all go to bed.
Male Voice Yes, yes, yes, yes.
Female Voice No, no, I — you — no.
Male Voice Yes, yes, YES.

They groan together in ecstasy, she still saying "No"

Piers Thank the Lord for that. (*He presses the remote control*)

It's a BBC 2, late-night Arts Programme

Female Voice But surely, the iconoclastic effect of the post-modernistic movement on the imaginative attitude of any creative artist who is trying to be taken seriously is a *disaster* from the point of view of any serious-minded commentator on the mores of contemporary ——

Piers turns the set off

Piers *Bollocks*. Bollocks, bollocks, bollocks squared and cubed.

Darren and Rosie enter. One of them turns on the lights

Ah, emeritus professor of How-To-Stack-Tins-On-Supermarket-Shelves has brought her star pupil safely back to the nursery. She will shortly be tucking him into his cot and wrapping herself round him for the night.
Rosie You rehearsed all that, didn't you?
Piers Yes. Have a drink.
Rosie No, thank you.
Piers How about the infant progidy? (*sic*)
Darren No, thank you.
Piers (*very friendly*) Ah, go on. Have one. (*He pours a largish Scotch*)
Darren I said no.
Piers (*proffering the Scotch*) Well say yes. Come on. Celebrate your Great Achievement in acquiring a brain.
Darren (*shrugging*) OK then. If you say so.
Piers Yeah? Really?
Darren Yeah.
Piers (*savagely*) Stuff it up your arse. Get your own. (*He drains the glass*)

Darren doesn't take offence, he just laughs, relaxed and in charge

Rosie You know that's really childish, Piers.

Piers (*imitating her*) That's really childish, Piers. (*His bitterness and anger is in full charge of him*) Not half as childish as destroying works of art worth a fortune.

Rosie Oh, no, Piers. Give it a rest.

Piers All our futures thrown away like that and you don't seem to give a toss. Is he so — wah, eh? Larissa didn't think that much of him. There's a great, big hole at the centre of all this that I don't get. It's driving me *mad*.

Rosie There's a lot you don't get, Piers, and never did.

Piers No, no, no, no, no, no, no. That won't wash.

Perhaps Darren starts to lead Piers off, but Piers just walks in a circle, getting away from him

Darren Go and keep your girlfriend warm, go on.

Piers You're used to it, aren't you? Living on the edge … you people … even Larissa … but I'm not. How can so much disappear? "Oh, that this too, too solid flesh would melt …" Every other bloody thing has.

Rosie Oh, Piers, go to bed for God's sake.

Piers (*imitating her*) Oh, Piers, go to bed, you're being embarrassing. All these feelings all over the place, tidy them up at once. Come on, up, up, up. (*Swaying, he mimes fussily tidying-up*)

Rosie Come on, darling. I think it's bedtime.

Piers Beddy-byes.

Piers starts to go but Rosie takes him by the arm and re-routes him

Rosie No, not that beddy-byes, this beddy-byes. Remember?

Piers suddenly hurls her off savagely

Piers I can take my bloody-self to bed.

Darren is instantly active, physically threatening Piers

Darren Oi. Touch her again like that ——

Darren is restrained by Rosie

Rosie It's all right, Darren.

Darren — and I'll smack all that gleaming bridgework down your throat. You're ——

Rosie Darren. Calm down.

Piers Gleaming bridgework. My. Aren't we literate and brave now I'm too pissed to stand?

Rosie (*very sharply*) Go to bed, Piers. *Now.*

All the energy drains quickly out of Piers

Piers All right, all rhgh', arigh'. I'm going. 'S a great life, innit? Got to apologize to Young Stud for living in my own home now.

Darren Better to be a young stud than fit for the knacker's yard.

Piers stops dead

Piers Ooh. Oh. Ah. (*He pulls an imaginary arrow from his heart*) A barb of wit. Noël Coward would have been proud of you. (*He dissolves into almost falsetto giggles as he collapses on to the sofa and passes out*)

Darren Has he died laughing?

Rosie This has got to stop.

During the following they move Piers on to the floor, pick him up and start to carry him out; Darren holding his arms, Rosie holding his ankles

Darren I didn't start all that.

Rosie We both did. Months ago. Come on, help me get him to bed.

Darren His firm goes up the spout, and they can't pay her mortgage, that's all my fault? Huh. I'm the only one bringing any money into this place.

They put Piers down briefly on the floor, still holding his legs and arms

Rosie The moment has come, I think, to produce those paint ——

Darren Sssh. (*He drops Piers's arms and quickly checks to see that Larissa isn't about*)

Rosie He can't hear. He's out of it.

Darren He's not the only one.

Rosie Anyway, the moment has come. It's crunch time after all, isn't it, for you and me?

Darren Whaffor?

Rosie You — you're free to go now.

Darren I've always been free to go. (*He picks up Piers's arms again, standing astride Piers's head*)

Rosie I mean, you don't need me any more.

Darren pauses, shocked. He drops Piers's arms again

Darren You trying to get rid of me?
Rosie All right, then. Let's turn it round. What is there to keep you here
  now?

*Darren is trying to cope with the idea, the fear even, that he is no longer
wanted by Rosie*

Piers Oh, God, I'm in the Blackwall Tunnel.

Darren moves away and Rosie puts down Piers's legs

Rosie You've had your revenge on them. And now a nice, really rather
  sophisticated joke turns into — my God, look at him. What a free fall.
Darren What do *you* want me to do?
Rosie Oh, come on, Darren. Don't slough off responsibility for your
  actions on to me.
Darren (*upset*) I can't answer what I want until you tell me what *you*
  want.
Rosie We're at a crossroads — hah — to coin a cliché. You've got a great
  job in Swindon, and commuting to Swindon will soon lose its glamour.
  So. Sooner or later you'll have to move.
Darren You can commute *from* Swindon, too.
Rosie Sorry?
Darren Well, I'll be working five, six days a week and you only work
  four, so …
Rosie Are you suggesting I should come with you?
Darren Yes.
Rosie To live in Swindon? With you?

*This, of course, is what Rosie wants most and she cannot keep the
emotion out of her voice, which confuses Darren*

Darren Well, *no*, not if you don't want to.
Rosie (*laughing, embarrassed*) Well — yes — no — you decide.

*Darren is trying to gather his scattered, shattered emotions. Piers,
when he speaks, sounds quite clear and pleasant in between being
incomprehensible*

Piers Big Issue. Get your Big Issue here. [My bank manager does not
  have married parents]. (*He subsides again*)
Rosie We'd better get him into bed.

Darren Rosie ... Rosie ... these last six months have been the happiest time of my life. You've brought me out into the light really. You don't understand 'cos you've always lived there. You have to — well, make that journey to understand what ——

Rosie To coin another cliché ——

Darren Jesus, Rosie, I can't finish a sentence ——

Rosie Sorry, it was that bloody journey that everyone's making.

Piers You were always sort of frigid with me, Rosie.

Darren Oh, no.

Piers 'S a terrible put down. 'S tha what you always longed for? A bit of rough?

Rosie Oh, God, this is hopeless.

Darren That's it, isn't it, Rosie? I'm just your bit of rough.

Rosie Is that what you think?

Darren Well, OK, but I've been ... happy ... totally happy. (*He shrugs, at a loss*)

Rosie And so have I, richly so. That's why I'm asking you — no both of us I suppose. What now?

Darren Yeah.

Pause. Rosie decides she must take the initiative

Rosie Well, obviously, you've got to move to Swindon.

Piers groans

Things decide themselves, don't they.

Darren (*desperate*) But we can keep in touch?

Rosie Oh, Jesus, Darren. Keep in touch. Spare me that.

Piers D'you think you could help me up. I seem to have lost the use of my legs ...

Darren, who would rather throttle him, grabs him, grabs his hand and yanks him up

Darren Here.

Piers Aaah. Oooa. Oh, I — (*Seeing Darren*) Aaah, 's Darren the dildo. Leggo me.

Piers pushes Darren away

Larissa enters, sleepy, in a dressing-gown

Larissa Oh, Weetie, what are you doing? (*She hurries to him*)

Piers Aaah, Goddy, the light of my life.

Piers falls against her; she can't hold him

Rosie Quick, help her, Darren.
Darren Drop him on the floor.
Rosie Careful, Larissa. I've got him.
Piers (*maudlin*) And Rosie, the other light. I got two lights.
Rosie Darren, get behind him. Quick. Help.

As Darren helps, so Rosie ushers Larissa away

No, Larissa, we can cope.

Darren is left holding Piers for a moment

Piers He's after me now. He's insatiabub — urg.

And the words become garbled as he gently and half-deliberately slides down through Darren's arms, raising his own arms above his head so that Darren is left holding his sweater

He's undressing me now.
Rosie Come on, help. No, not you, Larissa.
Piers (*crawling off stage*) My mother said there'd be days like this.

Piers exits

Larissa Weetie.
Darren Oh, sling him in the river, that'll sober him up.

Darren throws Piers's sweater off after him

Rosie Bedtime, I think.

Rosie exits

Darren I could kill her sometimes. (*Nearly in tears*) I really love her but I can't handle her. It's like wrestling with an octopus.

Larissa watches him for a moment

Larissa I remember you telling me you loved me once.
Darren You got Droopydrawers now, incha?

Larissa He snores when he goes to bed pissed.

Darren Sounds really romantic.

Larissa It's not what I signed up for, though, is it? An old bloke and no money.

Darren Tough.

Larissa (*starting to whimper*) It's all right for you, innit? You can get away from her, can't you? I'm stuck.

Darren I do what I like.

Larissa Well, don't get her in the club then, like you did me.

Darren What?

Larissa cries more and more freely throughout the following

Larissa I really loved you. I only went with him 'cos he was rich.

Darren Eh?

Larissa You were no good, were you? Pedalling that bloody bike for tuppence an hour. I had to do something. For the baby. For Bumpy.

Darren (*pointing*) Are you trying to say that I'm the father of that — that?

Larissa Course you are. Couldn't be him, could it? They was trying to have a kid for years. He couldn't. Didn't she tell you?

Darren Yeah, but ... I didn't ... you did all this, dumped me, because of — that (*the baby*)?

Larissa Course I did.

Darren Why?

Larissa (*bursting out*) 'Cos I was scared, scared rigid. I didn't want him to grow up like you did — on an estate somewhere, nicking cars, doing drugs — I wanted to give him a chance. Ooh, bloody hell, there he goes again. Here, come and have a listen. See what your kid's up to in here. Come on.

Darren stands rooted to the spot

Come on. You scared?

Darren No.

Larissa You bloody did it.

Darren goes to her, reluctantly

Go on, put your hand on.

Darren does so, slowly

Darren God. He dunnalf jump about, dun'he?

Larissa That's nothing. Here, listen.

Darren uncertainly kneels down, as Rosie did earlier, to listen to Larissa's bulge. Suddenly Darren laughs

Darren Phaw, dear. What a racket.
Larissa Yeah, he's calling to his Daddy.

This goes home and Darren quickly backs away

Darren I reckon you're having me on.
Larissa It's easy enough to have it all checked out when he's born, innit? I'm willing to face that. Are you? Or you just going to piss off like your dad did with you?

Darren looks at her for a moment, then goes and kneels to listen again

Wonderful, innit? And he's all yours.

She puts her arms round his head and shoulders

Rosie enters

Rosie Oh.

Darren scrambles to his feet, guilty as hell

Sorry. I just — I wondered when you were coming to bed.

Silence

Fade to Black-out

SCENE 3

The same. About five the following morning

The lights are switched off. The curtains are closed, shutting out the very early morning sun

Rosie is sitting silently somewhere. We may or may not see her in the gloom

Piers enters. He is a crumpled mess, straight from bed in his underpants. He shuffles to the window

Piers (*shuffling to the window*) Oh God, oh God, oh God. Never, never, never again.

He opens the curtains and immediately reels away with a cry of agony as the full rays of the rising sun hit him, flooding the room with light

Aaagh.

The sun rises throughout the scene, a glorious sunrise

Oh, Christ, I've gone blind. (*He whimpers as he moves to sit down*) I think Fluffy's crapped in my mouth. [My teeth have gone soft.] (*Seeing Rosie and jumping out of his skin*) Aaahgh. (*Then he has a reaction to his reaction*) Oh, oh, oh, oh, my head … I nearly had kittens, you, sitting there like a Buddha. I thought you were dead or something.

Rosie doesn't answer

Whassup? Your bladder on the blink too? Oh, God, I feel frightful. Look at me: half man, half pissed. Why do we do it? Relief, that's what, from the ghastliness of it all. Just makes it ghastlier, dunnit? (*By now, he is slumped in a chair somewhere*) Bit early to be sitting there, isn't it? Or is it a bit late? (*A thought occurs to him which amuses him*) Oh, dear. Don't tell me. You and young Homo Erectus have had a — oh, well, I'm sorry. Just because I hope he disappears up his own orifice I don't wish *you* any — oh, my head … oh, death, death, death, come on, get me out of this.
Rosie He has.

Piers is lost for a moment

Piers What? Who has what?
Rosie Disappeared up his own … Darren has. Happy now?

Piers stares

Piers What's that supposed to mean?
Rosie Darren. He's gone. Left.

Piers is torn between pleasure and sympathy

Piers Left? Or did you kick him out?

Rosie A bit of each.

Piers What does that mean?

Rosie It means that I think he wanted to go but I helped him on his way.

Piers Oh. Oh, dear. I mean … ha-ha — er — sorry — um — is that good or bad?

Rosie How do I know? I'm not a moral philosopher.

Piers No, no, quite. Oh, well, it's an ill wind … Don't get me wrong, I'm very sorry for you, but at least the three of us get on better without — um — dare I ask — (*unable to keep the glee out of his voice*) — has he gone for good?

Rosie Looks like it.

Piers Ah. Oh. Yes. Well, sorry, old girl, but it's probably all for the best, you know. In the long ――

Rosie (*snapping very sharply at him*) Oh, *shut up*, Piers, can't you? Give your brains a chance to catch up with your mouth.

Piers is shocked, subdued and hurt at this, but decides to be gracious

Piers Yes, yes. Course. Sorry. Insensitive of me. Perhaps I'd better go back to … (*He is on his feet, ready to go*) Oooh, oh, dear. Shouldn't have moved so quickly.

Rosie Save it, Piers. She's gone too.

Piers What?

Rosie He's taken her with him. Or she's taken him, more like.

Piers You mean — ?

Rosie Yes. He's pissed off with your secretary. It's getting to be a habit.

Piers Bloody hell's teeth.

Piers hurries out

Rosie And a very nasty one.

Perhaps she sobs, perhaps something else, but she is near the limit of holding on to herself. But to hold on to herself is what she is determined to do

Piers returns, shocked and utterly confused. He has his trousers, which he eventually gets on after a few attempts

Piers She's gone.

Rosie You notice everything.

Piers She never said a word to me.

Rosie (*a brief laugh*) Ha.

Piers She's packed and everything.

Rosie She's a very practical girl.

Piers Bloody hell's teeth. She's about to drop — why on earth did she
…? Why did she …?

Rosie It's his.

Piers What?

Rosie It's his.

Piers What?

Rosie *It's his.*

Piers What are you talking about?

Rosie Bumpy is Darren's.

Piers Bumpy is Darren's. Bumpy is Darren's? (*He works it out*) Bumpy
is *Darren's*. No, he's not, he's mine.

Rosie Ah, well. You'd better check that with Larissa.

Piers D'you mean that she says he's his?

Rosie Or she.

Piers What?

Rosie She says he or she is his.

Piers What?

Rosie Oh. *It's* his.

Piers What?

Rosie *Larissa* says that *Darren is the father of Bumpy.* There. Try and
grasp *something*, Piers, before I go … oh.

Piers wanders about, confused

Piers Are you trying to say that I'm still … that I still can't … that ——

Rosie Looks like it.

Piers Good God. D'you know, I can't take all this in, Rosie.

Rosie I'm pregnant, too.

Piers What?

Rosie I'm pregnant too.

Piers You're pregnant, too?

Rosie (*nearly cracking again*) Oh, don't start all that again, Piers. I shall
scream.

Piers All right, all right, all right. Pregnant? By him?

Rosie Of course him. Who d'you think?

Piers No, no, I just wondered if perhaps — I wondered if it might have
been — well — me.

Rosie That would have to be the longest pregnancy in history.

Piers Oh. Yes, yes, of course. So … he's responsible for — Bumpy …
and now he's got you up the … and now he's pissed off with …

Rosie You've summed it up to perfection.

Piers Charming. Bloody charming. How d'you feel about it all?

Rosie Ecstatic, of course.

Piers So all those years of trying. It was me.

Rosie Unless she's lying.

Piers I'm shattered, you know. I'm really — very upset. After all those years, to discover that I *could*. And now I can't. What a frightful little bitch she is — to do that to — are you going to have it? This kid?

No answer

You are, aren't you?

No answer

Doesn't that go against all your principles? Population explosions and all that?

No answer

Aren't there five billion too many of us, or something?

Pause

Rosie I don't think one more tiny, little baby will make a lot of difference, do you?

Piers laughs quietly, but not maliciously

(*Stung*) Anyway, it depends whether one looks at the world situation or just the British one. From a demographic point of view we have a baby famine in this country. In about twenty-five years there will be more pensioners than wage-earners. Who is going to support us? Ergo. We need children.

Piers You will be my advocate on the Day of Judgement, won't you?

Rosie (*the merest smile*) No.

Piers Well, well, well. My wife is going to be a one-parent family.

Rosie Doesn't have to be one.

Piers What?

Rosie Parent.

Piers You mean *me* — be the father to *his* little ——

Rosie *I'm* its mother.

Piers Oh, wonderful. I'll be pushing a pram round the job centre, what an intoxicating prospect.

Rosie Won't you be the father, Piers? Isn't that what we always really wanted?

Piers Give me a minute, Rosie. I'm having to take rather a lot on board at one go, you know.

Rosie Poor Piers. I haven't heard any yowls of anguish yet that Larissa has gone.

Piers No, no, well, I expect that'll hit me in a minute … Frightful business, isn't it, all this pregnancy stuff? Blowing up — being sick — looking like the back of a … I never realized.

Rosie Now you've got it all again. From the beginning. Just when it was about to end.

Piers It's the poor wot gets the children all right. Even someone else's.

Rosie But we're not poor.

Piers Oh, really? You could have fooled me.

Rosie Look under the table.

Piers Hm?

Rosie Go on. Look.

Piers glances under the table

Piers So?

Rosie Taped to the underside of the table.

Piers Taped to the underside of the table? What is?

Rosie Just look.

Piers Taped to the underside of ——

Rosie Oh, Piers, just look before I hit you.

Piers gets under the table and scrabbles about

Careful. Don't damage anything.

Piers Bloody hell, bloody hell, you're right. There's something — it's — here — I … (*He has stripped the tape off and is emerging with one of the two paintings*) It's one of them. It's one of them. It's *safe*. It's — it's not even damaged. How — ? what about the other one?

Rosie All in good time.

Piers How come it's all in one piece? Come on, Rosie, what the hell's going on?

Rosie He used fakes, substitutes to whack you with.

Piers (*heaving with emotion*) The bastard. That sh — that f — the c — there is no adequate word. How long's it been there?

Rosie Since you and Larissa moved in. He liked to watch you sitting there, moaning about your luck while that was underneath.

Piers The shit — the appalling little ... you're well rid of him, Rosie. (*He lays the painting on the table*) Oh, it's beautiful, isn't it. Beautiful. What the flaming heck am I going to tell the insurance now? Who cares, we're *rich* again. Thank God. I always knew something was — and you joined in on this sadistic — Rosie, how could you?

Rosie Revenge. There was a certain entertainment value at first in watching you go through it.

Piers Oh, Rosie. Supposing I'd found it?

Rosie Darren thought that risk was part of the fun.

Piers How could you do that to me? To *me*? Your loving husband.

Rosie Perhaps you could get Larissa back now. Keep her in the manner to which, etc.

Piers crashes to a halt — for a moment only

Don't you want her?

Piers Well, she's carrying his ...

Rosie But suppose it's yours.

Piers Well, she says it's his and she should know. Oh God, my head. Oh, sod my head. Just look at that little darling. It's sublime, isn't it? What pleasure she's given us. The brushwork. A thing of beauty is a joy forever. Straight off to Sotheby's for you, my girl. Where's the other one, Rosie? I'm not joking any more.

Rosie Don't threaten me, Piers, or I *will* put your head through it.

Piers Well, that's all right. At least we'll have the pieces for the insurance this time.

Rosie What a lover of great art you are.

Piers I'll say. Passionate. (*He laughs, almost wildly. Then catches himself*) Just a minute. Young Gristlehead, are you sure he hasn't taken the other one with him?

Rosie It's in the loft. He knew you'd never go up there.

Piers The bastard. But he's just walked away from a fortune if he'd stayed with you. Why?

Rosie Perhaps he regarded being with his wife and child as more important.

Piers But you're pregnant too.

Pause

He doesn't know, does he? (*A sudden thought*) Don't tell him for Christ's sake. We don't want him back.

Rosie Don't we?

This worries Piers

Larissa knows.

Piers Oh, *no*. Well, she won't — she's not daft. But if he tells her about the paintings, she might — well, she's got no claim on me, so ...

Rosie Great, isn't it? You seem to be fireproof once more.

Piers Sometimes I don't understand you at all, Rosie. I really don't.

Rosie I find that hard to believe.

Piers Look, I know you're upset for the moment, but — well, that couldn't have lasted, could it? You and Young Legover: purely temporary. Any more than my feelings for wassername — er — the point is we've got our old lifestyle back. Better even. We're sadder and wiser, but better. You can go on working at Amnesty and Greensleeves until you have the — er — it. Then we can afford a nanny and all that and then there'll be prep school to pack him off to and bingo, we're in clover. (*A new serious thought*) Oh, you'd better start having some pretty good medical attention. At once. I mean, one thing I learned about pregnancy lately is that if a woman past *thirty* starts her first child they call her an Elderly Primip. And well, *you're* past ——

Rosie I know how old I am.

Piers Yes, quite, well. You must — *we* must see that everything is — well — tickety-boo, mustn't we? We don't want any — um — no.

Rosie I was so happy yesterday I couldn't believe it. Larissa said it was nature, hormones. They make your brain go soft when you're pregnant. I could use a few more right now.

Piers Yes, it's funny, isn't it? How the body works. My headache's completely gone. D'you fancy a cup of tea?

Rosie Yes.

Piers I'll put the kettle on. You just rest there for now, old dear. Leave everything to me. Can I get you an aspirin or anything?

Rosie Piers, if you go on like this for long one of us is going to an early grave.

Piers Ha-ha. That's my Rosie.

Rosie Have you enjoyed yourself, Piers, these last nine months?

Piers Enjoyed? Oh, Rosie, show some compassion; I've been through the mill, you know.

Piers goes into the kitchen

Rosie Yes. You've experienced the whole gamut of human emotions. You've gone from rigorous self-satisfaction through unrelenting self-pity back to scrupulous smugness. It's been a humbling sight.

Piers returns from kitchen

Piers What on earth did you ever see in him, Rosie?

Rosie Everything. I love him to pieces. Into tiny little bits.
Piers Really? Then why let him go?

Piers goes to kitchen

Rosie At first he wanted to tell me everything. He *had* to tell me everything. That's young love; I remember. So, he brought it all to me like
a puppy with a sock. It was wonderful. I had my adolescence all over
again. But then he discovered there were some things he just couldn't
share with me. The gap was too big, he was already falling out of love
— no growing out of his — of his what? His obsess — no, his need.
And he didn't yet know it. So, I got out on a high. Now he thinks he
loves me. I like that. Soon he would have known that he didn't. Maybe
never had, he had just needed me for a while. He'd start to feel guilty,
to wriggle. Oh, I remember watching you, Piers. I couldn't face all that
again.

Piers enters

Piers You'll feel better with a nice cup of tea. My word just look at that
light out there. Just like a Turner, isn't it? I'm going to get up regularly
at this time. Amazing. He had them right here under my nose; who the
hell does he think he is?
Rosie That's just it. He doesn't know. (*She nearly cracks again*) He's still
making that sodding journey.
Piers I think I'll just pop up into the loft for a minute, just to ... well, see
that everything's ...
Rosie And miss this glorious sunrise?
Piers Oh, that, yes. Hm. Kettle's nearly boiling if you want a cup of ...
I won't be long.

Piers goes to the spare room as Darren enters

Darren Rosie, I'm in a complete — I can't think without you.
Rosie Where's Larissa?
Darren Asleep at her mum's.
Rosie You mean you've dumped her back with her family?
Darren She ain't got no family. Only her mum. Her dad pissed off years
ago. Same as mine.
Rosie And now you're doing the same to her?
Darren I couldn't sleep thinking about you. Help me. Please. I've never
been in love before, not like this.

Rosie I do get 'em, don't I? What with Piers and you. Fathers? You couldn't look after a cage of white mice.

Darren (*fiercely*) I looked after you, though, for months, didn't I? And you loved it.

Rosie Yes.

Darren embraces her. She responds. He tries to kiss her, passionately

No, no, no, nothing like that. Just hold me.

Darren I know you don't give a toss about me, except for — but, I ...

Rosie Except for what?

Darren Well, you know. I can't say it.

Rosie Say what?

Darren I feel like some daft girl. It's humiliating.

Rosie *What* is?

Darren You only want me for one thing.

Rosie stares at him in astonishment. Then laughs — at herself, not him

See? I knew you'd laugh.

Rosie How can we so misunderstand one another? You've missed the point ——

Darren — as always. Don't say it.

Rosie Well, don't keep missing it. Listen, Darren, since you went I've sat here feeling as though the world had ended.

Darren can't believe it for a moment. Then he tries to embrace her again but she refuses

But, you see, it hasn't.

Darren What?

Rosie Ended. The world.

Darren Mine did. Last night.

Rosie Rubbish. *The dawn.* Look at that. You're still part of it. We both are.

Darren Oh, bugger that. It was right in my eyes all the way here.

Rosie If you came back here to find out if I loved more of you than just your body then you have. I do. I love all of you ——

Darren — and me you, Rosie. Always ——

Rosie — but I'm staying here with Piers. No matter what you do.

Pause

Darren OK, I know. And I can't leave Larissa and Bumpy, can I? Anyway, I *won't* leave 'em.

Rosie I reckon you've passed all your exams since you came here. Every one.

Darren You passed a few, too.

They smile for a moment then he runs to her and hugs her

Oh, Rosie.

Rosie Yes. Just hang on to me for a bit. That's it.

Larissa enters

Larissa Hallo, Darren.

Rosie It's all right, Larissa. There's nothing to worry about.

Larissa No?

Rosie No.

Piers enters

Piers Rosie, the key to the trapdoor's not on the hook and I can't — (*He sees Darren*) What the bloody hell are you doing here? Get out.

Darren How would you like a smack in the gob?

Piers Oh, lovely. That's what a Diploma in Business Studies does for you, is it? Negotiation by left hook.

Larissa closes the door. Piers sees Larissa and is astonished

Piers Good Go — What do *you* want?

Larissa Thank you for the welcome, Weetie.

Piers No, no, I didn't … I thought you'd buggered off with the walking sperm bank here?

Larissa Oh, Weetie, I owed it to Bumpy. He needs his daddy.

Piers Whoever that might be.

Rosie The key to the loft is taped to the frame of the trapdoor, you'll see it when you go up the ladder.

Darren Don't break your neck.

Piers Don't you need me here, Rosie?

Rosie Just go and get your painting. We'll sort this out between us.

Larissa Painting?

A moment, reactions

What painting?

Piers Oh, just some old thing I've got up in the loft.

Rosie Yes, Larissa, it's one of the Turners. They're both safe. It was all a trick.

Larissa Oh, Weetie. Then you're rich again. (*She throws her arms round him*)

Piers (*fed up*) Like bloody magic, isn't it? (*He disentangles himself*)

Larissa That's brilliant. I'm so happy for you. I needn't feel guilty now.

Piers (*offended*) What?

Rosie Piers, go and get that painting. Leave this to me.

Piers Yes, yes, right.

Go to page 67 for Version 2 ending

Go to page 67 for Version 2 ending

VERSION 1 ENDING

Piers exits

Larissa Well, that's him sorted.

Rosie Darren, would you do something for me?

Darren Anything.

Rosie Go and see that Piers doesn't fall off that ladder.

Darren Anything but *that*.

Rosie Please.

Darren (*going reluctantly*) Give him a shove, more like.

Darren exits

Rosie D'you really not want Piers, not even with the money?

Larissa Not with twenty Turners.

Rosie And you do want Darren?

Larissa I must've been mad. But he's yours. You only got to tell him about ... (*She gestures*) He'd have to choose then.

Rosie And that would be dreadful for him.

Larissa I know who'll come second.

Rosie So I can trust you to keep quiet then.

Larissa Aren't you going to tell him, ever?

Rosie Let's get him used to Bumpy first.

Darren enters

Darren He's up in the loft playing a passionate love scene with the other painting.

Rosie Can he get down?

Darren I reckon he'll float down he's so happy.
Rosie Lucky him.

Larissa has a contraction

Larissa Aaaah. Darren, it's starting. Bumpy's on his way. You got to get
  me to the hospital.
Darren What? On me crossbar?

Rosie moves to the phone

Larissa My minicab's waiting downstairs.

Darren ushers her out, doing her breathing exercise to encourage her

   Larissa exits

*Darren stops at the door and runs back to Rosie. They have a wordless
moment*

   (*Off*) Darren.

*Darren goes as Piers enters, carrying the other painting and blowing
dust off it*

Piers There we are my precious. Did the nasty man lock you in the dusty
  loft then? Oh, have they gone?
Rosie Yes.
Piers Good. Saves me throwing him down the stairs. (*He puts the
  painting down*) Right, my darling, you sit there and take the weight off
  your feet and I'll make us all a nice cup of tea.

   Piers exits, still talking

   (*Off*) D'you fancy a spot of toast with it? And some of your mother's
   chunky marmalade?

Rosie is alone, c

Rosie I don't think I could eat, I feel a bit queasy … Oh, God of course.
Piers (*off*) We might wander into Sotheby's, just to see what they say.
  Then I think I'll go and see my bank manager for a couple of words;
  the second one'll be off.

Piers goes on talking as the lights swiftly fade to Black-out

(*Off*) Pompous, po-faced, pin-striped bastard won't know what's hit him ...

CURTAIN

VERSION 2 ENDING

Piers starts to go then remembers the painting and returns for it, grumbling all the way

Piers Wouldn't like anything to happen to this. You turn your back for one minute and paintings disappear and reappear, your wife gets up the duff, your girlfriend tells you it wasn't you, the world turns upside down ——
Darren What did you say?
Rosie Oh, Piers. Get out.
Darren (*stopping Piers*) Hold it, Ferret Face, I want you.
Piers (*hiding behind the painting*) Go on, punch a hole in that. I'll see you get ten years.
Darren What did you say about Roise?
Piers That she's ... (*He realizes*) Oh.

Silence

Rosie I think that's what's called a pregnant pause.
Darren (*to Rosie*) Are you? (*To Larissa*) Did you know this?
Rosie Yes, I am. Now for God's sake let him go, Darren. Then we can discuss this. Calmly.
Piers (*laughing*) Calmly? Leave me out of it, will you?

Piers exits, with the painting

All look at each other, not sure where to go next

Darren And you weren't going to tell me?

Silence

What a dirty trick, Rosie.

This hurts her

Rosie You'd made your decision. With Larissa.
Darren But you've got my kid in you. Our kid.
Rosie So has she.

Darren stares at her for a moment, then turns suddenly on Larissa

Darren Ferret Face is rich again.
Larissa I've had enough of him, even with twenty Turners.
Darren Yeah. Don't blame you. (*He is near tears*) This is unbearable. I love you, Rosie.
Larissa Well, which of your kids are you gonna dump, then, Daddy?

Darren is unable to answer

Darren (*eventually*) Neither of 'em.
Rosie What?
Darren I ain't dumping neither of them. I'll never dump a kid of mine. And don't either of you ever try to make me.
Rosie Are you suggesting ——?
Darren Yes. I am.
Rosie —— that we … (*she points to each of them in turn*) together?
Darren For our kids. None of this is their fault. Have you got a better idea?

Rosie thinks for a moment

Rosie (*finally*) No.
Darren There.
Larissa You know what my mum'd say: it'll all end in tears.
Rosie She's probably right but perhaps that's better than beginning in tears.
Darren (*surprised*) You mean you'll do it?

Rosie doesn't answer

Rissa?
Larissa Well … I dunno.
Darren Ah, go on, Rissa. For all of us.
Larissa Well … if Rosie …?
Darren Great. Rosie?
Rosie If Darren chooses you, Larissa, you know he'll hate you for making him leave me. And if Darren chooses me he'll grow out of me anyway … one day. So, at least it's logical.
Larissa Oh, yeah. One mustn't forget one's logic.

Rosie I've just spent four hours contemplating life without you, Darren, and I think I'd rather be part of a three-parent family — at least for now. So … if Larissa …

Larissa Hear that, Bumpy? Looks like you're going to have two Mummies. Aren't you — aaah. (*Suddenly she is convulsed with pain*)

Rosie }   { What is it?
Darren } (*together*) { What's the matter?

Larissa It's happening. Bumpy's coming.

Rosie runs to phone

Rosie Quick. Take her, Darren. We must get her to the hospital.
Darren What, on me crossbar?
Rosie Lay her down, you idiot. While I get an ambulance.
Darren Oh. Yes. Course.

Rosie is dialling as Larissa groans on and Darren mimes her breathing exercises to encourage her

Meanwhile, Piers enters with both paintings

Piers What's all the noise about?
Larissa Aaah.
Darren She's having Bumpy.
Piers Oh, my God. Not in here.
Rosie (*into the phone*) Ambulance, please. At once.
Piers Somebody call an ambulance. Quick.
Rosie Oh, shut up, Piers. You'd better get a wonderful price for those Turners. We're going to need every penny.
Piers What? Brandy. Brandy. We need some brandy.

Rosie gives instructions quietly into phone

Darren You can't give her brandy.
Piers Not for her, for me.
Darren I'm going to be a father, Ferret Face. Isn't life great?
Piers No wonder there are five billion too many of us.
Rosie (*hanging up*) Do you like this place?
Piers Here? Love it. Why?
Rosie It's all yours. We're going to Swindon.
Piers All three of you?
All Yes.
Piers Together?

All Yes.
Piers What on earth d'you want to go to Swindon for?
Rosie Love.

*Piers's reaction. Larissa moans and Darren embraces Rosie as the lights
swiftly fade to Black-out*

CURTAIN

FURNITURE AND PROPERTY LIST

ACT I
SCENE 1

On stage: Dining-table. *On it*: solicitor's letter
4 dining-chairs
Sofa. *By it*: TV dinner
Coffee-table. *On it*: telephone, copy of *Yellow Pages*
Drinks cabinet. *In it*: various bottles including Scotch, glasses
TV
CD player
2 late-period Turner paintings on wall
Window curtains open
Front door bolts and security chain fastened

Off stage: Clipboard, pen, bottle of cheap champagne in plastic gift carrier
bag with ribbon and card (**Darren**)

Personal: **Darren**: rucksack containing napkin
Piers: doorkey, wallet containing £300 in banknotes

SCENE 2

Strike: 3 glasses, bottle of champagne and wrapping, tea mug, banknotes,
napkin

Set: Doorkeys on coffee-table

Re-set: Door chain unfastened

Off stage: Hairbrush, make-up (**Rosie**)
Tray containing 3 cups, saucers and spoons (**Rosie**)
Pot of tea (**Rosie**)
2 unframed Turner paintings (**Darren**)
Black bag, scissors, Stanley knife (**Darren**)

Personal: **Rosie**: doorkey, wrist-watch
Larissa: handbag

ACT II
SCENE 1

Strike:	Tray, cups, saucers, spoons, pot of tea
	Black bag
	Scissors
	Stanley knife
	2 fake damaged paintings and frames
	2 unframed Turner paintings
	Hairbrush
	Make-up

Set:	Items to reflect **Larissa**'s taste
	2 letters on dining-table
	4 knives, forks, napkins on dining-table

Personal:	**Piers**: doorkey
	Rosie: doorkey, handbag containing prescription in paper bag
	Darren: doorkey

SCENE 2

Set:	TV remote control on sofa for **Piers**
	Window curtains open

SCENE 3

Set:	Rolled-up Turner painting taped to underside of dining-table
Re-set:	Window curtains closed
Off stage:	Trousers (**Piers**)
	Painting (**Piers**) (Version 1 ending)
	2 paintings (**Piers**) (Version 2 ending)

LIGHTING PLOT

Property fittings required: nil

Interior. The same scene throughout

ACT I, SCENE 1. Autumn early evening

To open: Daylight from window, gradually fading as scene progresses

Cue 1	**Rosie** switches on the lights *Snap on lighting*	(Page 2)
Cue 2	**Rosie**: "Just leave me alone." *Black-out*	(Page 22)

ACT I, SCENE 2. Autumn afternoon

To open: Daylight from window

No cues

ACT II, SCENE 1. May early evening

To open: Daylight from window

Cue 3	**Piers**: " … we get this place." *Black-out*	(Page 46)

ACT II, SCENE 2. May evening

To open: Night light from window, TV flicker effect

Cue 4	**Piers** turns the set off *Cut TV flicker effect*	(Page 47)

Cue 5   **Darren or Rosie** switches on the lights   (Page 47)
               Snap on lighting

Cue 6   Silence   (Page 54)
               Fade to black-out

ACT II, Scene 3. May dawn

To open: Gloomy interior, early morning sunrise from window

Cue 7   **Piers** opens the curtains   (Page 55)
               Snap on bright lighting, sunrise effect increasing as
               * scene progresses*

Cue 8a   **Piers** (off) "Pompous …"   (Page 67)
               Swift fade to black-out (Version 1 ending)

or

Cue 8b   **Darren** embraces **Rosie**   (Page 70)
               Swift fade to black-out (Version 2 ending)

EFFECTS PLOT

Please notice on page 76 concerning the use of copyright music and recordings.

ACT I

Cue 1	To open *Classical music from CD player*	(Page 1)
Cue 2	When ready *Door entryphone rings*	(Page 1)
Cue 3	**Rosie** gets up *Door entryphone rings*	(Page 1)
Cue 4	**Rosie** switches off the CD player *Snap off music*	(Page 1)
Cue 5	**Rosie**: "I'll lose the number." *Door entryphone rings idiosyncratically*	(Page 11)
Cue 6	**Piers**: "It's — it's wonderful." *Crash from bedroom*	(Page 15)
Cue 7	**Darren**: "… what people are gonna do." *Door entryphone rings idiosyncratically as Cue 5*	(Page 24)

ACT II

Cue 8	To open Scene 2 **Television Voice** *as script page 46*	(Page 46)
Cue 9	**Piers**: "Oh, sod off." **Television Voices** *as script page 46-47*	(Page 46)
Cue 10	**Piers** presses the remote control *Switch to* **Female Voice** *as script page 47*	(Page 47)
Cue 11	**Piers** turns the set off *Cut* **Female Voice**	(Page 47)

MUSIC

A licence issued by Samuel French Ltd to perform this play does not include permission to use any copyright music. Where the place of performance is already licensed by the PERFORMING RIGHT SOCIETY a return of the music used must be made to them. If the place of performance is not so licensed then application should be made to the Performing Right Society, 29 Berners Street, London W1.

A separate and additional licence from PHONOGRAPHIC PERFORMANCES LTD, 1 Upper James Street, London W1R 3HG is needed whenever commercial recordings are used.

MADE AND PRINTED IN GREAT BRITAIN BY
LATIMER TREND & COMPANY LTD PLYMOUTH
MADE IN ENGLAND